I Visited Europe and Survived

A travelogue of fun and adventure

Jan Frazier

Outskirts Press, Inc.
Denver, Colorado

Outskirts Press, Inc.
http://www.outskirtspress.com

ISBN: 978-1-4327-1749-0

Outskirts Press and the "OP" logo are trademarks belonging to Outskirts Press, Inc.

PRINTED IN THE UNITED STATES OF AMERICA

Dedication

This creative nonfiction book is based on true experiences – no matter how unbelievable, hilarious, and inconceivable they may seem. There are a sprinkling of fictional episodes, but 99 percent of the adventures were real. The book definitely wouldn't have been possible without the companionship of **Dee Delmastro Shaub** and **Karen Smith** as well as hundreds of students and adult travelers with whom – during a thirty-year span – I have had the privilege of traveling abroad.

Part of the joy of living is laughing, so I hope that you are able to laugh your way through this book and see the light side of traveling to Europe – it's a side that only an American traveling in a foreign country can comprehend. In addition, I hope that you can enjoy reading about the awesome sights plus the well-preserved history, which are available in the incredibly beautiful countries of Europe. Enjoy!

Acknowledgements

As always, I want to thank my two dear friends for helping me proofread and edit. They are two English teachers who are unsurpassed in their field – Paul Pearson and Karen Smith. Both spent many years in the classroom as well as in the Counselors' Office at Pekin Community High School, and literally thousands of Pekin students remember them as being "the best" in their field.

Table of Contents

Introduction

The dark near-midnight sky was filled with rain. The storm was starting to dissipate around the Chicago area as Dee and I sat on the plane at O'Hare. It was 11 o'clock and in half an hour, we were supposed to have landed in London. As it was, we passengers on the plane were just getting into queue on the runway for the second time that evening. We were restless, tired, and hungry. Since the electrical storm was now breaking up, it looked as if we might finally take off.

My legs were propped over my chartreuse carry-on, which sported a multitude of travel stickers. It had been stuffed under my seat earlier, but sometime during the recent hours, I had retrieved cards from it to help pass the time. The stewardess hadn't asked me to push it back under the seat, so I used it as a prop, letting my legs dangle over the carry-on's plump body.

A week earlier, Dee and I still had plans to spend our summer vacation in Arizona. Being second-year teachers with three months off, we both yearned to travel. Getting out of the Midwest was our goal as the cornfields lacked the excitement we sought.

As TWA, Flight 164, got into queue, I glanced at Dee who was reading a novel she had purchased earlier in the airport. I closed my eyes and sat back. It was our second trip abroad; with fantastic memories of the previous year, we could hardly wait for the adventures of the next nine-week journey.

Letting my mind relax into a half-reverie, I thought back to the past week when our plans were suddenly changed from traveling west to Arizona to going east to Europe.

Chapter 1

We're Going *Where* on Vacation?

It was a sizzling hot, scorcher of a summer in 1972. Records were being broken all across Illinois. Plans for traveling west for a vacation the following week were quickly subsiding – if it was hot in Illinois, then the heat would be unbearable in Arizona.

I sat next to my open bedroom window, lace curtains billowing in the air from the hot, summer breeze, and looked at my gaudy, chartreuse-colored carry-on luggage. The bag had been on sale at Sears, and I couldn't imagine why someone hadn't bought it. As if the neon color didn't draw enough attention, as an added attraction, I pasted brightly colored travel stickers on the baggage. Rome, London, New York, San Francisco, Paris, Amsterdam, Chicago, and Lucerne decorated the fat, bulky body of the bag. It stood 2 ½ by 2 ½ feet – no standard, international sizes in those days. Long chartreuse handles stuck straight up to complete the "look." It was ready for travel, but I wasn't positive to where.

"Hey, Dee," I said after hearing her bubbly voice on the other end of the phone line. Undoubtedly, she was still in her bathrobe, trying to comb her black, naturally curly hair. Her real name was Dominica Francesca Delmastro – a real Italian name – but her friends all called her Dee. Dominica just didn't fit a tiny little thing like her.

"Oh, J.J. I'm glad you called. After I get dressed, I'm going shopping at Carsons. What exactly should I buy for our Arizona vacation?" she asked, cheerfully. Dee was always upbeat, seemingly with no cares. Her ability to talk – with or without her hands – came from her Italian heritage. Well, maybe the trait was just from her father, who talked nonstop. Dee and I had been planning a trip to Tucson for months now. I fell in love with Arizona my freshman year in high school when my parents and I made the long three-day trek by car through the Southwest.

The first glimpse of the Tucson desert buffeted on one side by the incredibly beautiful, purple Catalina Mountains was all I needed – I literally invented reasons as to why I needed to return to Tucson.

"The desert in December is much better for my sinuses than the cold, damp Illinois weather," I pleaded to my parents. "I'd love to practice my photography on the flowering cactus at Easter," or "The University of Arizona is offering a great course on Milton this summer. Bradley doesn't have it, and I'd love to take it. What do you think?" My parents finally fell for that one and let me go to summer school at the U of A in 1969 with the agreement that I'd live with my Aunt Mildred, my dad's sister.

But this summer – 1972 – found temperatures being broken all across the United States, and it was only June. The beaches were already packed with tourists trying to escape the city heat, and cabins and wooded resorts in the North were booked for family vacations.

I was flipping through *Travel Leisure*, looking for a mountain resort where we could stay cool, horseback ride, and hike. The desert – as much as I loved it – was unthinkable.

Maybe we could go to Colorado – Estes Park would be nice. In the middle of the magazine was a huge centerfold of the most spectacular mountains that I had ever seen – a white paradise of snow-covered Alps in the midst of Switzerland. As I turned the page, another centerfold opened to pictures of fairytale castles and medieval fortresses in Germany and royal, lavish palaces in France. By the third large centerfold page – showing incredible English cathedrals with spires reaching to the sky, gargoyles overlooking the entrances, and mosaics and gilded frescoes in the

2

sanctuaries – I was hooked.

Mustering up the courage to tell Dee that there might be a change of plans, I cradled the phone in my sweaty palm. "Well, you'll need some nylon pants and jacket in case it snows, an umbrella because it can be very rainy, and a skirt in order to enter the churches."

"Snow – umbrella? Wait a minute. I need these things for Arizona?" she asked, confusedly. Certainly, there was reason for her bewilderment.

"No, you need them for Europe," I stammered. I decided that I may as well be direct with her.

"For Europe? Did our plans change while I was asleep last night?" Dee asked slowly, now more befuddled than ever.

"Sorta," I replied with a weak laugh, trying to decide how to continue. "Well, the TV says that there's a heat wave across the United States. It's incredibly hot in Arizona – 120 degrees." I was known for being spontaneous and having spur-of-the-moment mind changes. It drove Dee crazy.

"Here's what I was thinking – you know, our ten-day tour of Europe last year was great but too short. We only saw a couple of large cities. What about getting Eurail passes and *really* exploring Europe on our own? We have a little more than nine weeks until school starts. The U.S. dollar is still up in Europe, and airfare is down."

The silence on the other end made me realize that my spontaneity might be too much for Dee this time.

"We could spend the next few days planning our once-in-a-lifetime, nine-week excursion across Europe. What do you say?" I concluded.

"I love the idea of Europe, but do you really think we could do this on our own? You know, we were with a tour group last year. Do we know enough to go alone?" Dee's questions expressed sincere doubt.

"Sure. Why not? We've been abroad once. What could

3

go wrong?" Boy, was I naïve.

"Well, Jan Hoyt, I'd like to think that I'm game for anything," Dee answered, her usual, agreeable manner taking hold once again, "but this is all so sudden. I mean, I thought we were heading out West."

"Jan" was a name that I seldom heard unless I was in trouble with my mother. I was seldom called anything but J.J. by my friends. Even though my mom had named me Jan, she called me Jay from the start. When I was just learning to talk and finally mastering the "J" sound, I was so proud of myself that I always said it twice, so my name became "J.J." Well, that stuck throughout elementary, high school, and college with many of my close friends.

Dee and I had just completed our second year of teaching. She taught fourth grade, and I taught high school. We both felt that we had gained useful knowledge for the classroom from the previous year's ten-day, whirlwind tour – it had been fantastic.

Every play we saw in London was a theatrical possibility for my classroom. After seeing *Julius Caesar* on stage, I was determined to have the students act out a few scenes to bring the play to life in class. The following spring, I borrowed togas from the Latin Club; the conspirators brought "cloaks" that they could pull about their ears to hide even from the night, and Brutus stabbed Caesar with a cardboard sword as he uttered "Et tu Brute." It was a fun experience for the students, and an event that I would recreate each spring when we read the play.

Dee brought back a variety of postcards from London, Paris, and Amsterdam, to make collages of each city to use in her social studies classes. Getting vacation brochures from the local travel agent, she let the students use her collage as a model as they scissored apart the brochures, creating their own fabrications of their favorite European city.

While in Europe, Dee also found some dolls that were dressed in traditional costumes. She bought them, displaying them on a shelf in the classroom. Anything unique was an added bonus when it came to learning.

Now, a nine-week journey would, undoubtedly, be incredible. How many more classroom ideas could be gleaned from our experiences abroad this year? And – in the '70s – a trip abroad was a great tax deduction for a teacher.

"I already checked flights yesterday afternoon," I added, trying to sound nonchalant.

"Oh, so you didn't just *now* come up with the idea." Dee managed a giggle so I knew that she wasn't truly upset.

"Well, no," I answered sheepishly. "First, I found these fantastic pictures of German castles, the Swiss Alps, French palaces, and English cathedrals in a travel magazine, and then I decided just to check on fares to Europe." I paused, hoping for a comment from Dee. There was none, so I continued.

"I found cheap tickets on airlines leaving from Chicago, and we can get seats for next Wednesday. Also, Eurail passes are a good buy, so we can hop a train anywhere in Europe, getting on and off as many times as we want," I added, all in one breath, proud of my initial, thorough investigation.

"Are you sure this is a good decision?" Speculation creeped into Dee's voice once again.

"Sure, I'm sure."

"Well, you know I'm not a good organizer so you'll have to plan everything," Dee replied.

I could tell that Dee was weakening and that I was winning. When Dee started talking about me planning everything, it was a good sign.

"I can do that. What do you say, Sport?" Including the word "sport" was a sure clincher.

"Okay, J.J., let's do it. Hey, I have to get off the phone now. My sister wants to use it. Talk to you later." I heard a hasty click on the other end, reminding me that one of Dee's teenage sisters was probably glaring at her.

The Delmastro household was a continual circus with fourteen children, and one of the children – usually a teenager – always needed the phone. Being an only child, I actually enjoyed the lively commotion – or rather complete chaos – at the Delmastro house. Often during the past few years, I visited the Delmastros in the evenings. Dee and I would join into the conversation or activities of some of the children, and if one group of kids wasn't doing or conversing about something interesting, we just moved to another group. Somewhere in the household, intriguing things were happening.

I didn't know Dee from childhood. We met in college and formed an instant bond. Opposites usually attract, and our family backgrounds were certainly totally different. She was from a large, extended family of Italians and was involved in many family activities. Her dad ran a local, family-owned restaurant. Dee had early training as a waitress, earning money for college as well as her own personal expenses. Many evening activities were curtailed with "Sorry, have to go, J.J. The restaurant calls."

I was an only child. My spare time could not be used working at a part time job – I needed to study. I was a nerd, I guess, because my life seemed to be focused on continually striving for A's in college – there was no room for other priorities.

My father, who was a banker, always stressed that B's were fine. "Don't forget that a social life is important," he would grin. "I never got straight A's," Dad would say. "In fact, I nearly flunked out of physics at the U of I my junior year. No one is the wiser today. *You* don't have to get all A's, J.J." Even though my dad was my idol, I trusted his judgment only so far, and B's just couldn't become a part of my vocabulary.

Actually, my grandmother used to tell me that Dad always struggled in school, trying to get A's but didn't often succeed. Dad was really quite a character, and Grandma grimaced as she told of his tipping over an outhouse on Halloween night, its occupant sitting there stunned. "It was just kids' stuff," Dad would say. "Art Ball and Jacob McCallahan were my best friends, and the three of us really didn't know that Mr. Moss was in there." Dad would laugh, his hearty good-natured chuckle, his body shaking.

In contrast to Dee's Italian heritage, my mother's family was German, and all the women had hips measuring fifty inches. I continually said silent prayers about my own destiny when looking at the broadsides of my aunts. I wanted my father's physique; even though he was short, he was slender. In fact, both of my parents were short which always caused people to wonder how I became 5 feet 7 inches, tall for those days. Oh, well, I didn't care as long as my hips didn't measure three feet across like my German ancestors.

Because of Dee's Italian background, she too worried about her hips. With pasta included at every meal, she continually had to battle extra inches and pounds, which no one noticed after seeing the beautiful jet-black curls that framed her face. My fly-away, straight strawberry blonde hair was always a problem – a ponytail was a natural solution. Always thin, gangly, and the tallest in the class, I longed to be petite and dark like Dee. In addition, I longed for Dee's fun, carefree personality because I was more serious and, I suppose, organized. Organized was not even part of Dee's vocabulary. I was always in charge of coordinating any important, pressing plans, and she established the fun activities. I guess that made us a good team.

Later that afternoon, I reserved our plane tickets and Eurail passes, then browsed through the latest edition of *Europe on Five Dollars a Day*. Nowadays, five dollars a day is inconceivable; five dollars might pay for half a dozen trips into a public toilet. However, in those days, it was possible. We could get a room for three dollars a night and shop at grocery stores for our food, costing a grand total of two dollars. Yes, it was all a possibility.

Our itinerary was well on the way to being choreographed – England, Holland, Germany, France, Spain, Switzerland, and Italy. "A Taste of Europe" would be an apropos name because we would get a taste of one city – maybe just a whiff – before moving on to another. But we'd definitely get to see highlights across the entire continent in nine weeks.

"Dee, things are all planned," I said, calling her later that night. I had the whole itinerary set up – typical of my compulsive behavior of not ending a job until all aspects were completed.

"We'll start in London, and then it's on to Holland. That was your favorite country last year. Maybe the Dutch have had time to carve more wooden shoes to replenish their stock. Remember, last summer you bought thirteen pairs for your brothers and sisters!"

"Well, yeah, I did get a little carried away," she answered, chuckling as she remembered cramming thirteen pairs of wooden clogs into her suitcase.

"We'll continue across Europe to Germany, then down to France and Spain, and finally end in Switzerland."

"Hey, wait a minute!" Dee chimed in. "What about Italy? My grandparents were from Italy. We *have* to go there."

"Oh, sorry, no time for Italy. Our flight departs from Zurich," I spewed quickly, now waiting for the explosion on the other end.

"Hey, wait a minute, J.J. That's not fair–"

"Just kidding, Dee – last is Italy. Our flight departs from Rome."

"Not funny, J.J." Relief sounded in Dee's voice as she giggled, "Okay. That's terrific. Whatever you plan is fine with me as long as you include Italy."

"Pack for warm days and cool nights in Holland; hot days and hot nights in Spain and Italy; wet days in England; snowy days in Switzerland's mountains; and anything in between for Germany," I concluded, grinning to myself.

"That's impossible!" she exclaimed.

"Listen, Dee. Just don't over pack, but take clothing for all types of weather, and we'll search for launderettes," I commented hesitatingly, knowing that finding any place to do laundry was nearly impossible in Europe. The previous year we had found *one* in England and that was by luck.

"Well, talk to you tomorrow," I concluded. "Start practicing your Italian. *Arrivederci.*"

Neither of us had any concept of the ridiculous adventures, filled with fun and a great deal of personal growth, that lay ahead in the next nine weeks of traveling abroad. It was the summer during which we visited Europe and survived.

Chapter 2

Rendezvous with Barbara

It was mid-June. The previous few days had flown by – shopping, packing, planning – and before we knew it, Dee's younger brother, Dave, was driving us to Chicago's O'Hare in his beat-up, red Ford Coupe. Driving through the cornfields of the Midwest, heading north, Dee and I chit-chatted in the back seat as David tapped his fingers on the steering wheel, keeping time to Elvis.

"You girls sure you'll be okay traveling alone for the rest of the summer? How will you survive in the countries that don't speak English?" Dave asked as he turned down the radio. He was a dark, gorgeous 20-year-old Italian-American with wavy, black hair and had a quiet, soft-spoken voice.

"We'll be fine. We have our French, German, Spanish, and Italian dictionaries," I answered with confidence. We had books of infinite knowledge with us, I thought. What could possibly happen? Dee and I had the word "naïve" written across our faces – let me say no more.

"Can you pronounce the words in all those languages?" Dave continued, throwing me a glance through the car's rearview mirror.

"Don't be silly. All we have to do is point to the word, David. Now, quit worrying," I replied, puffed up with the idea that we could conquer all.

"Hmmm" was Dave's only comment as his gaze returned to the road. Obviously, he wasn't as convinced as we were that our trip would be trouble-free.

I had always had a "bug" to travel and seemed to be fearless – invincible, actually. My dad had always encouraged me to "give things a whirl" and traveling was one of those things. I was sure the trip would be perfect with no problems.

"Gosh, it doesn't feel as if we're going to Europe," Dee remarked, trying to change the obviously touchy subject. "Maybe, it's because the plans were thrown together so quickly. A week ago, we were planning a trip to Arizona," Dee remarked, flashing me a grin.

"Don't say it doesn't feel as if we're going to Europe. That's bad luck," I retorted. Perhaps, we should have realized *then* that this was a foreshadowing of the 36 hours to come.

We arrived at O'Hare and bid Dave goodbye.

"You girls be careful, and don't forget to write," he called as he pulled away, his car sputtering as he accelerated.

Waving as we lifted our suitcases, we walked toward the airport terminal. We each had a carry-on plus one large wheel-free piece of luggage – no luggage on wheels in those days. They were bulky, heavy, and cumbersome – no way to walk gracefully carrying them.

By now, my newly acquired European travel stickers had found their way onto my larger brown bag. Because that piece of luggage actually looked normal, I felt it too needed to be recognizable on the baggage carousel. In addition to the stickers, a jumbo hot pink ribbon was tied onto the handle. I knew now that I couldn't miss my bag – nor could anyone else.

In those days, lines at the international ticket counters were long because European flights were relatively inexpensive – approximately 300 dollars for a round trip. Because the dollar was strong in Europe, Americans could afford to fly to London in December to do their Christmas shopping on an extended weekend and return home for work on Monday. We could get full-course meals for two dollars and entrance fees into museums were a mere fifty cents. Plus, in 1972, the extravagant, European VAT tax –

12

Value Added Tax used in most European countries today – had not yet been added to merchandise so everything was dirt-cheap for Americans. Italian leather purses cost five dollars, and French perfume sold for around seven dollars. American tourists in Europe had a heyday bringing home bargains.

We waited in line an hour at TWA, rocking from one foot to the other as we inched our way up to the counter. Finally, it was our turn. We got boarding passes together, which assured us a seat next to each other.

Security checks were not a problem in those days – no hijackers, terrorism, or bombs with which to contend. At least we weren't publicly aware of them although they undoubtedly existed. We were whisked through the simple security-check formalities as we looked for Gate E 8. Quickly finding it, we sat, chatting excitedly and munching on ham sandwiches and drinking cokes.

"I'm sure that I'll spill something before I even get on the plane. I'm so sloppy, you know," I commented, brushing crumbs from my light blue pantsuit. My mom was a terrific seamstress and had made an array of matching pants, skirts, and tops for the trip to Arizona, which I now had packed for Europe. They were all fashioned in that fine, unforgettable, wrinkle-free polyester knit of the '70s. It was the first non-wrinkling material the world had ever seen so no matter how ugly the polyester patterns were, everyone loved it. Even the men had "leisure suits" made of polyester. They, also, were ugly – no, atrocious.

My mother loved to sew for me and had always designed all my clothes, making me the envy of my classmates throughout elementary and high school. In those days, hand-sewn clothes were much more fashionable than store-bought merchandise, and I always felt fortunate to have a mother who spent hours at the sewing machine, creating the latest fashion for me. At any rate, the matching clothes that she had especially created for this trip were all wash and wear – good for sloppy people like me.

My thoughts returned to a night that Dee had spilled an entire plate of spaghetti in her lap during her break at her family's restaurant. Short on time, her father wouldn't allow her to go home to change, and she donned a full-length apron, continuing her work. She wanted to cry.

Still, Dee hadn't attained the degree of sloppiness that I had and probably never would. I had the uncanny ability to drip food on my clothes during the first bite of a meal. Even food that couldn't possibly drip, such as sun dried raisins or beef jerky, would somehow create a spot on my blouse when dropped. It was uncanny.

We chit-chatted for an hour, and as our boarding time neared, we grew leery.

"Dee, I haven't seen any flight attendants or pilots pass through the gate."

"I've noticed that, too. Maybe, our flight is just a little late," Dee remarked optimistically.

Late wasn't exactly the proper word. *Postponed indefinitely* was more on target. At exactly 4:30, we were supposed to have boarded; instead, a sugary-sweet voice came over the intercom.

"All passengers for Flight 164 leaving for London, please report to the main terminal. Your flight has been postponed."

The lady's voice would have been more correct if she had said, *Run as fast as you can to beat the crowd. Get your butt onto another flight because your plane is going nowhere.* Perhaps, then, we would have moved more quickly.

I looked at Dee who was sporting a grimace. I grabbed my chartreuse carry-on with the multitude of travel stickers. A half dozen additional pictures and names of European cities – purchased after we definitely decided to go abroad – glossed the sides of the bag. I had given no thought that I looked like a true American tourist with this unsightly, gaudy green hand luggage. It could be seen for three blocks and may as well have had a neon sign flashing "gullible American tourist."

We started on our mile-long hike to the terminal. At this point, our luggage was still lightweight in comparison to its heftiness at the conclusion of the trip. However, at the time we didn't know this, and we were slow in sloughing the bags through O'Hare. By the time we got to the main terminal, two million people were ahead of us. An hour later when we finally got to the ticket desk, *all* flights on *all* airlines leaving for London were full.

"Please have a seat, girls," the ticket agent said curtly. She looked frazzled, with her brown hair straying from her tightly pulled bun. Her black, plastic-rimmed glasses slid down her nose as she nervously pushed them up when she talked. It was then that I noticed that the lady was a little strange – she had one green eye and one blue one. I glanced down at her airline nametag – it read "Barbara."

"Your flight may still take off. It is currently postponed," Barbara stated matter-of-factly. "Check with me in an hour," she snapped, quickly pushing her glasses up as perspiration gathered on her nose. She was obviously tired of dealing with the hoards of people from Flight 164, all trying to escape O'Hare.

I hesitated at the desk for a moment as Barbara glared at me and then proceeded with her mounds of paperwork, building by the minute because of the cancellation. Her nerves seemed to be getting the best of her as she sweated through the decisions that had to be made.

A half hour passed and then an hour. It didn't look as if our plane was going to depart or that we would be blessed with any other flight. Tired of seeing us at the desk with our hound dog looks, Barbara was diligently trying to book a flight for us.

Influencing her quest more than our looks was my irritable tone. "Look, we have reservations in a London hotel tomorrow night. We need to leave tonight, *Barbara."*

15

She glared at me in astonishment, trying to decipher how I could possibly have known her name. My eyes glanced down at her nametag, and she grinned sheepishly.

"Okay, girls, I'm still searching for a flight. Please have a seat and be patient," she stammered, trying to adjust her bun now completely askew on the back of her head. Her glasses had totally disappeared, probably thrown on the floor in a moment of frenzy.

Again, we took our seats, frustrated. Within fifteen minutes, however, our names were called, and we shot from our seats, tripping over our carry-ons and garbage that now cluttered our sitting area.

"Girls, I have a flight for you." Barbara looked excited as she motioned for us to come closer to the desk.

"Great!" Dee exclaimed, all-too-eager to hear the details.

"Well, it's not *exactly* what you wanted," Barbara continued, hesitantly. "You will fly into Poland first and then catch a connecting flight to London. I'm sorry, but there's no room for your luggage."

"What!" I exclaimed. Dee silently looked at Barbara in horror.

"No, listen to me, *Barbara*." I made sure to stress her name just to be certain that I had her full and undivided attention. "We're *not* going to Poland, and we're certainly not going without our *luggage*. You must be kidding!" I exclaimed, using my best assertive "teacher voice." I looked directly into her green and blue eyes – Barbara wasn't kidding.

Undoubtedly, my face was red from the rise in my blood pressure, and I continued rather loudly – actually, I was shouting, "Look, we'll wait until 7:30, and if the flight is still postponed, we want a room for the night." I finished in a firm voice, hoping my point had been made clear. Barbara nodded, obviously hoping we would just return to our seats.

My patience was waning, and I knew that tolerance had

never been one of my strong points. My mother had always said that I'd never have children because I wouldn't be able to wait for them to finish their meals, get dressed, or even go to the bathroom. My constant on-the-go personality allowed little time for R and R. And yet I had patience with all of my students, continually going over grammar rules until they got them right. When reading *Romeo and Juliet*, I gave a fifty-quote test at the end, which required daily review as they struggled through the Elizabethan language. By the end of the three weeks spent on reading the play aloud, I had reviewed the fifty quotations with them dozens of times, feeling assured most of the students were prepared. And they were! Even so, patience in general was not my strongest asset, and tolerance with Barbara was losing ground quickly.

At 7:30, there still was no flight, and I made my way to the desk to speak again personally with my now-intimate friend, Barbara.

"Barbara, we would like a room for the night, please," I said in a pseudo-sweet voice. "We are not waiting any longer." I flashed her a full smile as my voice again took on an assertive tone.

"Yes, of course, ladies. Let me see what I can do." Barbara knew that she had lost the battle and now proceeded to find us a room with no argument. I felt a real sense of accomplishment.

As it turned out, Barbara – or rather the airlines – provided us with a nice room at O'Hare's Best Western, plus two meals for each of us. Some passengers from Flight 164 chose to wait, hoping desperately that the flight would depart that evening. Fortunately, we had made the right decision because at midnight, the tired travelers that were still lingering in the airport were informed that the flight was cancelled until the next afternoon. Exhausted, disappointed, and dejected, they made their way to the hotel for a well-deserved hot shower and a soft bed.

When we checked into the hotel, it was 8:30, and we ordered dinner to be brought up to our rooms. After a hot shower and a change into my PJs, I sat munching on the salad and chicken sandwich as I watched television. My mind returned to another time when my flight had been postponed. I had been coming home from Arizona with my cousin. We sat in the airport for three hours because of the plane's faulty interior door. Eventually, the door was described to the waiting passengers as being "repaired." Nervously, I boarded the plane with the thought that it probably wasn't a door at all but rather a loose wing on the plane or a faulty, leaking gas tank. I decided not to discuss my fears with my cousin, who was on her first flight from Arizona to Illinois. Silently, I was wondering if a wheel had fallen off or if the brakes had gone bad on Flight 164 to London. I'd never know.

At any rate, TWA did agree to pay for a phone call to our hotel in London so we could inform them that there would be a one-day delay. The London hotel assured us that it would be no problem, and our room would be waiting for us. At least one aspect of the trip seemed to be working in our favor.

The following day seemed interminably long. Dee and I shopped in the airport stores, buying *The Chicago Tribune, Newsweek*, and crossword puzzles to pass the time. Barbara was nowhere to be seen at the check-in desk. Still disgruntled that she had been willing to put us onto a flight to Poland without our luggage, I had hoped to harass her just one more time before leaving.

Finally, the clock showed 4:30, and the moment arrived to board. Flight attendants and pilots had been filing onto the plane since 4:00 so that day's flight would not be a problem – or so we thought.

However, at that moment another unlikely obstacle was occurring, which would delay our flight still another seven hours.

Chapter 3

Bon Voyage at Last

We boarded Flight 164 exactly on time. "No postponement now, J.J," Dee noted, enthusiastically. "In forty minutes we'll be on our way to Europe."

Passing time, we researched the in-flight movie schedule and dinner menu, which were the important things in life at the moment. Later, we could relax and try to nap. From 4:30 until 6:00 we were in denial, thinking we would leave at any minute. However, by 6:15, admittedly, we were late, and an uneasy feeling began to overtake us. My stomach began to knot, and my mouth felt like cotton. I could feel my nerves getting edgy, and I looked at Dee who was biting her nails. The pilot assured us, though, that the plane would be leaving soon, and we silently lived with our fears.

It wasn't until 6:30 that the pilot gave us the unforgiving news, "This is Captain Nicholas Dimopolus. I'm sorry to inform you that an electrical storm over the East coast is delaying take off. Planes are being re-routed to avoid the severe weather conditions, hindering Chicago's air traffic. Unfortunately, there are many planes in line before us, and we will have to wait our turn. We apologize for the delay."

I looked at Dee, thinking that was the extent of the bad news. I started to say something when the captain continued. "Unfortunately, food and drinks cannot be distributed until we're in the air. However, water can be served. Also, we extend our apologies for the air circulation on the plane. In order to conserve fuel, the air- conditioning cannot be initiated. Thank you for your co-operation." The captain said this in one swooping breath, obviously, eager to get off the intercom.

19

"That's it? This must be a joke!" I exclaimed. No, it was true. As I looked over my shoulder, I saw everyone gaping out of the windows in an attempt to count the dozens of airplanes lined up ahead of us – Air France, Lufthanza, Pan Am, British Air, KLM. Captain Nick was kind enough, however, to keep us posted at fifteen-minute intervals in order to maintain our hopes of departure.

Slowly, we were inching our way up in line – our hopes building as one plane after another lifted into the night sky, taking an alternate flight route toward the East coast. Finally, at 8:15 we were close to departure. "There are two planes ahead of us, and we should be airborne in fifteen minutes. Thank you for your patience." The captain's voice had a more optimistic, cheerful ring to it. I smiled, glancing out the window as dusk and rain clouds darkened the sky.

"It was worth the wait, I guess," Dee sighed, sitting back into her seat. "At least, we *are* going to leave tonight."

There were sighs of relief throughout the plane with excitement mounting at the prospect of leaving. I was still looking out the window. For some odd reason, the knot in my stomach had not dissolved.

"Remember, yesterday you said that you didn't feel as if we were going to Europe? How are you feeling about that tonight?" I asked, hoping Dee's answer would quiet my unrest.

Dee didn't have a chance to reply as Captain Nick interrupted once again. "I'm sorry to inform you, but the electrical storm is now right outside of Chicago, and O'Hare has been closed. We are forced to return to the terminal. However, in order to retain our place in line, no one will be able to disembark. I'm really sorry for the inconvenience."

"What? This is unreal!" Dee screeched in disbelief.

Someone in the back of the plane yelled, "Hey, Captain Mondipopolos, get this stupid plane in gear and get its dead butt off the ground." A rumble of irritable moans could be heard throughout the plane.

"I just can't believe this" was all I could say. For once, words seemed to escape me.

Still more incredible, once again no food or drinks were available, and no air-conditioning could be activated. Women searched their purses for snacks, and men rummaged through their carry-ons. With no air-conditioning, the air was stuffy and warm. It was an edgy, restless, bloodthirsty crowd on that airline for the next two and a half hours – a crowd that was on the verge of losing control with the thought of mutiny.

From my chartreuse carry-on – which was a bit too large to fit under my seat no matter how hard I squeezed and crammed so I literally stuffed it into the overhead compartment – I pulled out a deck of cards. We tried to focus on a game of "Crazy Eights." When the game dried up, we retrieved our crossword puzzle magazine that we had purchased earlier in O'Hare, and we worked together on some puzzles. Eventually, we returned once more to the card game – time dragged.

I turned to look at the other passengers. Some had their heads down on their empty food trays in an attempt to rest. Mothers were trying to quiet screaming babies, and restless toddlers ran up and down the aisles. Others had head sets or books to pass the time. One passenger must have brought his own liquor as he offered water glasses full of booze to his neighbors. They seemed to be the only people on the entire plane who were laughing and enjoying themselves.

Now, as I sat listening to the people around me, I pulled myself back to reality now and glanced at my watch – 11:20. It was then that we heard the familiar voice from the back of the plane, "It's about time that we're moving, Nicky boy, because my fuse has just burned out. I'm a heavyweight wrestler, you know, and on my way to..." We didn't hear the rest of the sentence; perhaps his companion shut him up. I wondered if he had gotten a few glasses of the Jack Daniels from the passenger across the aisle.

Rain still hit the window, but Captain Nick had now informed us that the electrical storm had completely lifted, and weather was clear all the way to the East coast. At 11:50, our plane finally lifted into the night sky, amidst a crowd of cheering, exhausted passengers. We had departed for Europe at last. In the years to come, I would take high school students abroad for the summer, and with each trip, I would think of this incredible nightmare on the runway of O'Hare. I always breathed a sigh of relief when the plane would take off, not wanting to go through an escapade like this with forty students aboard, who were all eager to get their first view of the Eiffel Tower, Buckingham Palace, or the Colosseum.

By 1:30 in the morning, dinner was served. Most of the people on the plane were asleep, too exhausted to eat. Even though Dee and I were tired, we were also ravenous, quickly downing a plate of chicken and noodles, roll, and fruit.

Usually, falling asleep was difficult in the cramped conditions on the plane, but that night was an exception. Within minutes after the dinner tray was removed, I was asleep. I heard nothing for the next four hours, and at 6:30 the next morning, the flight attendant had to wake me for breakfast.

With all the chatter and commotion, it was evident that everyone was starved. Looking around, I noticed that it looked as if a tornado had hit the inside of the plane. Newspapers, cups, candy wrappers, magazines, and even diapers cluttered the aisles. The plane was literally trashed.

The next hour went by quickly as we ate and attempted to freshen up after our long entrapment. We changed our watches to London time – now 1:30 in the afternoon – and tried to act chipper. Finally, we landed safely and lined up for foreign customs.

"The line is short this year," I commented, thinking of

the long customs' line the previous year.

"Well, there isn't any other American flight coming into the airport at this time of the day. Remember, all *normal* U.S. flights arrive by 8 a.m.," Dee mentioned.

Dee was right – our time had been spent on Chicago's runway, and the flight should have arrived during the airport's busiest hours – early morning.

Quickly, we moved toward the booth where the man dressed in a navy blue government suit was stamping passports. He asked how long we would be in England as he glanced at our passports. His eyes casually fell on my neon-green bag, and he removed his reading glasses to get a better view. He opened his mouth to say something but must have had second thoughts. He stamped our passports, and we were done in a total of sixty seconds.

We went to the baggage carousel to collect our checked luggage. I always had a fear that my bag wouldn't appear. The previous year in London, my fear had come true. My luggage didn't arrive on the flight from Paris, and I had to wear the same clothes for two days. Dee's pants, which were a size too big and four inches too short, just didn't work. None of her blouses that were clean matched my pants so I gave up the quest for clean clothes and donned my dirty apparel until my bag appeared. This year, though, I packed a change of clothes in my carry-on, just in case.

Fortunately, both of our bags arrived in the midst of the hundreds of others. I was so glad that I had thought of the huge flamingo pink ribbon because I spotted it immediately as my suitcase tumbled onto the carousel. While waiting for Dee's luggage, a little girl – probably four or five years old – busied herself looking at my gaily-colored travel stickers and plump bright green bag. Looking back, I'm horror-struck that I ambled throughout Europe with such a monstrosity.

We put our four bags onto an airport cart and headed

for the international exit, which would lead us to the main airport terminal.

"What a breeze," Dee said. "Let's splurge and catch a taxi into London. We're both exhausted and don't know our way around well enough to take the – what's the underground in London called?"

"Tube," I answered.

"Oh, yeah, the tube. Besides, battling the hundreds of commuters on the tube wouldn't be fun with all our luggage in tow," Dee continued.

"You're right. I'm game for a taxi. I'm really glad we got some English currency before we left Illinois. At least, getting money exchanged here at the airport isn't a worry after all we've been through. It seems as if we departed a week ago." I yawned, feeling the lack of sleep, plus jet lag.

Tugging our bags – which seemed even heavier today than the previous day – to the airport taxi stand, we hailed a taxi. The driver helped us as he, too, eyed my unusual carry-on, glancing up to see what the owner looked like. Too tired to wonder what he was thinking, I slumped into the back seat, unable to cover my exhaustion.

"Where to, lasses?" the driver asked with his cockney accent.

"I can't remember the name of the hotel. Just a minute, please," I replied, searching through my purse. "Here it is," I said, handing the driver the hotel's name and address.

While I tried to make small-talk with the driver, I heard Dee trying to stifle her giggles. Looking at her out of the corner of my eye, she sheepishly raised her hand, which contained a silver-colored, broken door handle.

"I closed the door, and the handle just fell off," she whispered, amid her laughter, which was no longer being suppressed.

"Geeze, Dee. Try to put it back." I glanced at the taxi driver, who seemed engrossed in watching the airport traffic.

Dee fumbled with the broken handle as I attempted to engage the driver in light conversation. Glancing at her several times, I noticed that she was still struggling. Finally, she shot me a meek grin and gave me the "thumbs up" that it was fixed. Whether it would actually function, I didn't know.

"You on holiday, girls?" the driver asked.

"Yeah, we're going to tour Europe this summer," I answered.

"Where you from?"

"The Midwest – Illinois," Dee chimed in. She was sitting back feeling smug over her door-handle accomplishment, but I was betting she was going to get out on my side of the taxi so as not to put the handle to a full test. Meanwhile, I reached for the ashtray to deposit a gum wrapper.

"Really? I lived in Chicago for a year. Great city," he answered, trying his best at a Midwest accent. "I couldn't drive a taxi though. Never got the hang of driving on the other side of the road."

"Yeah, I had forgotten how strange it feels to be on the wrong side," Dee smiled as we watched the driver quickly weaving in and out of the traffic lanes, dodging the hundreds of compact cars.

"Well, excuse me, miss, but I believe it's you Americans that drive on the wrong side," he chuckled as he threw us a quick glance in the mirror.

"Oh, you think so?" Dee giggled.

I was only half-hearing the conversation as my hand now held the ashtray which fell out of its encasement as I flipped the lid shut. It was me who was now stifling a giggle as I sheepishly held the ashtray high enough for Dee to view. Covering her mouth, Dee was making an attempt to muffle her laughter as I struggled to replace the ashtray into its holder. Miraculously the driver was unaware of the hubbub in the back seat.

We had entered the heart of London with traffic becoming congested. Hundreds of small, foreign cars vied for the right-of-way – or maybe it was left-of-way.

I heard Dee continuing her conversation and ask the driver where he had worked in Chicago, but my mind was starting to shut down from lack of sleep. I tried to follow the conversation of his working in a restaurant at the Sheraton Hotel, but I was just too tired. He was telling of waiting on Bob Hope one night, and as the nonstop jabbering continued in the background, I must have dozed off. The next thing I remember was Dee shaking me as the taxi pull up in front of a hotel. I fumbled for my purse so Dee and I could split the cost of the ride. The driver – now known as Felix to Dee – helped us with our bags.

"Great fun chatting with you two," he smiled, offering us his hand to shake. "I love Americans – such a good sense of humor, you know." Felix was attempting his Yankee accent again, which unconsciously gave way to his native cockney. "Cheerio, girls. Have a bloody good trip."

"Thank you," we said with a wave.

We grabbed our bags and entered the hotel lobby. Although it was a modest hotel with a small lobby, the scent of fresh gardenias filled the room. I was always amazed at the Europeans' love of beautiful, flowers, which were displayed in every hotel, banquet hall, and restaurant. We registered in record time and started to our room.

"At least, there's an elevator in this hotel. Last year's London hotel didn't have one," Dee commented as we sloughed our bags through the small lobby.

"True. In fact, we had only one hotel last year with an elevator. It kept us in good shape, though, climbing all the flights of stairs," I replied, smiling. "By the way, it's not an elevator – it's a *lift* in England."

"Oh, right. I forgot."

Our room was clean but small. It was typical of most European hotel rooms of the '70s. Nothing fancy, but they were spotless and certainly adequate.

A double bed with white chenille bedspread was located under a window, which opened unto a row of nondescriptive hotels across the street. A green over-stuffed chair in the corner had slightly worn arms and had seen better days. Two ivory and green flowered, oval carpets – typical floor coverings for the 1970s – acted as accent rugs over the shiny hardwood floors. Of course, there was a small table, which supported a large vase of red carnations and baby breath. Bathrooms and showers were down the hall and shared by the entire floor.

Because it was already mid-afternoon, we decided we would shop since – in those days – the stores all closed at 6:00. Besides, shopping would be a no-brainer. The day had already been exhausting and visiting museums was not at the top of our list. After shopping, we could grab a bite to eat and return to the hotel to retire early.

No maps of London were available at the hotel desk, but the receptionist gave us directions to Regent Street, a fashionable shopping area of London. The weather was perfect – bright, sunny, and warm – and walking to stretch our legs was great after being confined so long on the plane – a total of 16 hours.

It was an afternoon of window shopping, viewing the new European fashions that had not yet come to mid-America. We enjoyed observing the current shoes and dresses. Mini-skirts were still the rage, and the shoes being shown had pointed toes, not yet seen in Illinois. Bellbottoms were still being worn in Europe as well as in the States. Usually, the current European fashions would not reach the Midwest for a year or two after their appearance in Paris – the fashion capital of the world. Exhausted by 5:00, we saw a delicatessen. Not wanting to stray yet from American food, we grabbed chicken sandwiches, trimmed with lettuce and tomatoes, a side salad, and lemonade; our meal was complete. Still observing the rushed American eating routine, we gulped our food and in ten minutes, we were ready to head back to our hotel.

"Dee, let's get a taxi again. Hiking all the way back to the hotel doesn't seem like fun. It's probably an hour's walk from here since we've gone so far from the start of Regent Street, and I'm not even sure of the direction, now."

"I'm tired, too," Dee answered. "What's our hotel's name?"

Searching my purse for the name and address, I realized it had been left with our taxi driver from the airport.

"Well, let's see. It was the Sloane Hotel, I think. I looked at the name when we called from O'Hare to change our reservation. Gee, that seems like weeks ago." I was truly searching my brain by this time for the exact name of the hotel.

"Well, yes, I'm sure it was Sloane Hotel," I said, trying to act confident. Unfortunately, when handing the paper to the driver, I hadn't even looked at it. Silently, I chided myself.

"Okay. Hey, there's a cab," Dee replied, as she waved to the driver.

"Sloane Hotel," I said, again feigning confidence as we climbed into the back seat and collapsed.

We chatted about Dee's sisters, wondering what they were doing at the moment. It was noon back in the States, and she imagined them all sitting down to lunch. I could see a wave of nostalgia pass over Dee's face as she talked about Teddie, her favorite little sister who was six.

I was unaware of the direction our taxi driver was taking – and too tired to care. As he stopped the cab, he said, "Girls, here's the Sloane Hotel."

Scrambling to get the correct change, casually I glanced at Dee. She was staring out of the window, a bewildered – aghast is more appropriate – look on her face.

"This is not our hotel, J.J," she whispered anxiously. "Sir, is there another Sloane Hotel? This isn't the correct place."

I, too, was gawking at the building, which looked like a run-down, unkempt, skid-row dump. Long strips of paint had peeled off the windows, and the doorframe seemed to be hanging by one hinge. Unfortunately, the weathered sign above the door read "Sloane Hotel."

"Sorry, miss. This is the only Sloane Hotel in London," he replied, assuredly.

Desperately, I tried to suppress the lump that was rising in my throat and the tightness that was cramping my stomach. However, it was useless because panic continued to sweep my body as I realized I truly didn't know the name of our hotel. Worse yet, I didn't even know what it looked like or remember a landmark in the vicinity; all I remembered were non-descriptive hotels lining our street. How could I – *supposedly* organized and responsible – have neglected to remember details? Now, we were lost in a city of ten million people – and our luggage was in some unknown, nameless hotel.

Chapter 4

The Best of Britain

All we could do was pay the taxi driver and, apprehensively, climb from the cab. Standing in front of the Sloane Hotel, we were too dumbfounded to know what to do next.

"Can you believe that I was so stupid to leave the name and address of the hotel in the other taxi?" I again chastised myself.

"Don't berate yourself now, J.J. Let's go inside to see if the receptionist knows of another Sloane Hotel. You know, maybe the taxi driver was wrong," Dee added, trying to feign cheerfulness.

We opened the door, its top hinge hanging by a thread, and walked into the dimly lit interior. As our eyes adjusted from the bright sunlight, we looked through the din to see dark, worn furniture as a damp, dingy odor greeted us.

The small, elderly, white-haired man at the reception desk greeted us, displaying his frayed cuffs and a large toothless smile.

"May I help you, ladies?" he asked, pulling at his jacket sleeves that were not only totally threadbare, but also much too short, displaying shirt cuffs turned dingy gray.

"Well, we have a problem," Dee began as she relayed our sad, but true, story to him. He seemed to find some humor in what I believed to be a desperate situation. His chuckle turned into all-out laughter as Dee concluded the tale. To my horror, she suddenly saw the lighter side of the situation and began to laugh, too.

"Are you crazy, Dee? This is serious," I whispered. "We're lost, our bags are in an unknown hotel, and you're laughing!" I was appalled.

"Sorry, J.J., but this guy is funny," she whispered, suppressing another giggle as we turned away from him. "He's kind of pitiful, I know, but look at him. He's finding humor at life."

"Yeah, at our expense," I added hastily. "Sir," I pleaded, turning back to him, "please be serious for a moment. Is there another Sloane Hotel in London?"

"No, miss," he said, now trying to hide his smile after being chided. "However, I think there is another hotel with a similar name. Let's look in the telephone book."

He pulled out a well-worn phone book from under the counter and started to thumb through the white pages. Glancing at him through the dim light, I now noticed that his dingy shirt was missing several buttons. For a moment, I did pity him until I heard his stifled chuckle again.

"No, I was right to begin with – this little guy is *not* my friend, " I said under my breath. Actually the word "creep" started to enter my mind. However, I'd soon have to eat all my ill-thought words.

"Well," I heard him say, "there's Hotel Sloane on the Square and also Central Hotel Sloane. Do you think either of them could be your hotel?" he asked a bit timidly, still sensing my displeasure of him.

"Is one of them within half an hour's walk from Regent Street?" I questioned, hoping that might be a valuable clue, as I estimated it had taken us thirty minutes to walk to that area from the hotel.

"Hotel Sloane on the Square is in the southeast corner of London so that wouldn't be the correct one. Central Hotel Sloane could be a possibility."

Desperation sounding in my voice, I asked, "Could we, perhaps, call to see if we're registered there?"

"Yes, of course, miss. Allow me to dial the number for you," he added, once again revealing his smile, minus the teeth.

Dee talked to the person at Central Hotel Sloane, and by the conversation, it was evident that we had found the correct hotel. A sigh of relief followed her phone call.

"Well, we found it," she remarked. "It's about fifteen minutes from here."

"Allow me to flag a taxi for you ladies," our toothless hero added, as he exited the hotel to catch a cab.

"I've learned a lesson," I whispered to Dee as we followed the receptionist. "I need to double check to see if the hotel name and address are in my purse."

We shook his hand and thanked the receptionist repeatedly for locating the correct hotel. He seemed pleased that he could be of service. He waved as we pulled away in the taxi.

The driver – a native of London – chit-chatted about sights we should see. "Don't miss Westminster Abbey or the Changing of the Guard. And the pub next to the Guard House at Buckingham is a jolly good spot for fish and chips."

Dee – who still seemed oblivious to the crisis we had experienced – chatted amiably with the driver. On the other hand, I sat quietly, my mind flogged with hallucinations of weeks on the unfamiliar streets of London – no food, no clean clothes, wandering aimlessly in search of our hotel. Don't be delusional, I thought to myself. It wasn't *that* bad; yet I obsessed over my stupidity and the prospect of being truly lost in London.

In fifteen minutes, we arrived at our lost hotel and silently rejoiced. We paid our driver as he tipped his hat and zoomed off onto the busy London streets, filled with after-work traffic. I wanted to kiss the steps but refrained.

We tried to act as if nothing had happened as we walked past the hotel clerk, throwing him a casual smile. He bid us "good evening." We returned the greeting but hurried on, worried that he could read "Loser" all over our faces or simply see the large "L" plastered on our foreheads. Nonchalantly, we pushed the "Up" button at the elevator.

Going directly to our room, I still found it difficult to "unwind." However, at 10 o'clock after being up 35 hours with little sleep except on the plane, we both finally sank – no literally fell – into bed and tried to put our minds and bodies to rest.

"Wow, what a day," Dee sighed as she snuggled deeper under the down comforter.

"Three days, you mean. Our first evening was spent conversing with Barbara, remember?" I reminded Dee. "And the second night was spent on the plane."

"Yeah, that's true. But just think, J.J. We could have spent this morning getting acquainted with Poland," Dee replied with a chuckle.

"Yeah, well, it would have been fun to see Poland since we haven't been there, but *not* without our luggage," I concluded. "Let's get some shut-eye, Dee. I wonder what is in store for us tomorrow." No answer – Dee was already nestled into the soft, European featherbed, eyes closed.

* * * * * * * * * *

The following day, we visited all the usual tourist locations: Buckingham Palace, Changing of the Guard, Westminster Abbey, Tower of London, and the British Museum. My favorite sight, however, was Christopher Wren's inspiration – St. Paul's Cathedral.

Dominating a square mile, the cathedral was laid out like a Greek cross. I had seen pictures of the cathedral taken during WWII when London was in rubble, and St. Paul's stood virtually alone in the war-torn city. The fact that the church survived at all was a miracle since it received two Nazi bombardments early in the war.

The interior of the cathedral integrated the grandeur of great classical churches with Baroque sculptures, and its great gilded piers artfully disguised the supporting structures. An enormous, awe-inspiring church, St. Paul's

34

sported huge, domed arches, finished in gilded frescoes and fantastic, colorful mosaics. The beautiful, wrought iron-work created on the choir screens enclosed the intricate golden carvings of cherubs, fruits, and garlands overlooking the choir members. The one monument in the cathedral to survive the great fire of 1666 was John Donne's tomb. Totally intact, Donne's grave attracted hundreds of visitors every year. Many people going to see the grandeur of St. Paul's had the added surprise of finding his tomb, tucked away in a corner.

The vast interior of the church supported the Whispering Gallery Dome, an unbelievably huge, gilded dome weighing 84,000 tons. We climbed the narrow staircase consisting of 259 steps in order to reach the Whispering Gallery, a circular area halfway up to the summit of the dome.

"Dee, sit on the other side of the Gallery, and whisper to me. Let's find out if the acoustics really work," I said a bit skeptically.

As Dee whispered, it was incredible – every word could be heard.

"Wow! Wren must have been a genius to create this. What a masterpiece," I noted still looking at the architecture. "Let's climb to the top of the dome so we can see London."

Making our way up the winding stairs, which consisted of another 330 steps, it was possible to get a 360-degree bird's eye view of London from atop St. Paul's Cathedral. It was awesome. Tower Bridge, Buckingham Palace, Green Park, Westminster Abbey – everything was visible. Seeing the city from atop the cathedral gave us the layout of London as seen from an aerial view. A map pinpointed all of the highlights of London as well as lesser-known spots. Always in search of the out-of-the-ordinary sites, I liked roaming the crooks and crannies of the big cities. This year I wanted to visit Ye Olde Cheshire Cheese – a small inn frequented by Samuel Pepys, Dr. Samuel Johnson, Mark Twain, and Charles Dickens. I found it on the map, trying to cement into my mind which alleys and lanes to travel to find the inconspicuous, yet once popular hotel.

By late afternoon, we meandered into Covent Gardens – a chic shopping district but primarily the theatre area of London – in an attempt to snag theatre tickets for that night. Being lucky enough to fine inexpensive tickets to Shakespeare's *Midsummer Night's Dream,* we were thrilled.

As we left the ticket booth, I checked my watch. "We don't have time to return to the hotel to change clothes, but I think we're dressed okay, don't you, Dee?"

"Oh, yeah. Lots of people will be dressed formally, but we're both fine."

At the time, I didn't realize how out of place we looked – we were *so* American. Dee was sporting her red, white, and blue striped sailor top with a navy skirt. The wide stripes only accentuated her already full bust (which I totally lacked), and a polka-dotted headband topped her oh-so-chic outfit. Her bright red, patent-leather, over-sized shoulder bag was stuffed with everything imaginable – elephantine wallet, a dozen keys, a can of Coke, date book, five tubes of lipstick, mascara, eyeliner, liquid foundation with matching powder, combs, brushes, a half dozen hair curlers, notes from the final week in school, crackers, peanut butter, and a knife. There was no way she could walk through the crowds without plowing into someone with the bulging red monstrosity.

I, on the other hand, was dressed in an all-to-perfect, matching purple double-knit skirt and top – all sewn by my personal seamstress. The Europeans, all conservatively dressed in their traditional black, navy, or gray, did many double-takes on the two of us. At the time, I didn't understand that bright colors were strictly American; fitting in with the European crowd meant wearing something dark. It was only one of many lessons we were yet to learn.

"Let's just eat at that little café on the corner and then walk to the theatre. We should have plenty of time," Dee noted, "since we have almost three hours until the performance."

"Sounds good to me," I replied.

We decided to broaden our horizons and try something really English – traditional fish and chips – and we devoured twice as much as we should have. Since continental breakfast was always included in the price of the hotel room, we had decided to snack at lunch in order to conserve money – thus, the need for crackers and peanut butter from Dee's purse – and then eat one big meal at night.

Finishing our meal in two hours – record time according to the European schedule – we ordered coffee as Dee pointed to a crowd starting to form in front of the Royal Ballet It was a large, stately, white building with six columns supporting the marble sculptures, which were artfully placed across the upper façade of the porch.

"Wonder what's going on over there?" she asked more to herself than to me.

"Don't know. Excuse me," I said to the waiter, who was passing our table. "What's happening at the Royal Ballet?"

"Oh, the Queen's birthday is today, and she'll be arriving for the ballet in an hour."

We checked our watches – it was 7 o'clock – and we realized that we would have to decide between seeing the Queen or getting to our theatre on time.

"Dee, what should we do? Look, the red carpet is already rolled out."

Dee glanced to where I was pointing. "Gee, I didn't know there actually were red carpets. I thought it was just an expression," she grinned.

"Let's wait as long as we can without being late for our show," I said as I took my last sip of coffee and counted out some pounds to cover the bill.

Waiting until 7:45 and deciding that we didn't want to miss the opening of *Midsummer Night's Dream*, we left – quite downheartedly – without a glimpse of the Queen. Having made our decision, we walked briskly to The Theatre Royal Drury Lane at the end of Catherine Street in Covent Gardens. We were in the midst of the crowded West End, which was the theatre district of London, with some of the famous theatres of the city – Apollo, Aldwych, Palace, Prince of Wales, Garrick, and Whitehall. Marquee lights flooded the night, publicizing the performances. Hundreds of people dressed both formally and casually lined the sidewalks in front of the theatres, enjoying the evening air or awaiting entrance into the auditoriums. We arrived just as the curtain was rising.

The Theatre Royal Drury Lane was one of the oldest and most prestigious in London, built in 1812. Three theatres previously occupied the site; the first was built in 1663, burning down a few years later. Surprisingly plain on the inside, The Theatre Royal Drury Lane sported one of the city's largest auditoriums with various tiered balconies.

What a tremendous production. Both Dee and I were Shakespearean fans, and *Midsummer Night's Dream* was one of his funniest plays. This performance was a real hoot, and we laughed until we cried.

At intermission, as we got something to drink, I thought back about the first time that I had seen *Midsummer Night's Dream* on stage. It had been a college production, and a college friend of mine had played Puck. His devilish personality fit the part of Puck exactly, adding to the believability of the character on stage. Being the first time I had ever seen a live Shakespearean production, I was awestruck by the stage crafting, Elizabethan costumes, and characterization demonstrated in this one simple play.

The second half of the play drew the audience into the story as the three plots intertwined and Nick Bottom became an Ass, entangled in Titania's faery world; Lysander,

Demetrius, Hermia, and Helena were trapped by Puck's trickeries; and the hilarious "play within a play" was performed. The crowd roared and clapped at the conclusion, demanding several encore appearances from the actors, who waved and shouted to the audience in response.

"That was great!" I exclaimed to Dee as we descended the steps of the theatre, amidst the throng of theatre-goers, already pushing to reach the too-crowded subway. "Puck and Nick Bottom – Shakespeare doesn't get funnier than those two."

"Well, I don't know about that. How about Katherina and Petruchio in *Taming of the Shrew*?" Dee threw me a glance, eyes twinkling.

"Well, you've got me there," I replied with a grin. "It's a toss-up."

As we neared the Royal Ballet, a crowd still gathered.

"Hey, J.J., maybe the Queen is about to leave the ballet. That would be fate. Let's go see," Dee said. With her huge red purse slung on her shoulder, she bombarded her way through the spectators and seemed to pave the way for me, straggling behind.

"Your purse is literally a weapon, Dee," I whispered as we came to a standstill at the front of the crowd.

She blushed, trying unsuccessfully to flatten it to her side.

"Excuse me, sir," I said to a gentleman standing patiently at the corner. "Is the Queen expected to leave soon?" The distinguished looking middle-aged Englishman stood smoking his pipe, glasses sitting on his nose. He threw us a glance.

"Yes, miss. She's supposed to emerge within ten minutes. Look, there comes her chauffeur-driven car now," he answered in his perfect English accent as he pointed to the black Mercedes pulling up in front.

The crowd was jubilant – clamoring and jostling – as they waited for the Queen to appear, but we were amazed at the lack of police protection.

"You know, Dee, if the President of the United States were coming out, there would be tons of security. Amazing, isn't it? I guess, the Queen is so much a part of society and so loved that the thought of tight security isn't necessary."

The electricity of the crowd was nearly tangible as they waited. The legendary sedateness of the Brits seemed to be put in escrow for the night. Suddenly, they broke out into uproarious cheers as the Queen appeared at the door, royally bedecked in a chiffon dress, hat, shoes, and gloves in various shades of blue. Graciously, she waved that all-too-familiar royal twist-of-the-hand gesture as she basked in the swell of "Happy Birthday to You" struck up by the crowd. Their ecstatic cheers couldn't be contained as the Queen slowly made her way to her waiting car as she continued to wave to her adoring English audience.

The event had a strange intimation of an English family celebration, almost as though this was a private party to which we had been invited. Dee and I were singing with the British, and there was nothing rushed or pushy about the event – no onslaught of spectators being purged by police with cans of mace and no TV cameramen scrambling for a flawless shot. It was an at-home feeling of intimacy – spontaneity without mania.

Slowly, her chauffer-driven Mercedes inched its way along the narrow street as the crowd cheered their appreciation of seeing their beloved Queen. As cheers escalated, Her Highness gestured a royal wave to her audience, and several times the car stopped – once in front of us – as the Queen's perfectly-trained smile could be seen through the window. Dee raised her hand, trying to act *very* English with a slight wave to Her Royal Highness. I grabbed my camera for the perfect Kodak moment, and wouldn't you know, I had run out of film. Not only had I flubbed the chance to wave to the Queen, but I also had missed snapping a picture of our once-in-a-lifetime experience. And so

I let my camera hang uselessly around my neck as I watched the black Mercedes drive out of sight.

* * * * * * * * * * *

The next day, we took a bus to Stratford-Upon-Avon, stopping at Shakespeare's birthplace, his grammar school, church, and Anne Hathaway's House. Stratford-Upon-Avon was a mecca for thousands of visitors a year, with its half-timbered houses and gorgeous flower gardens, budding every conceivable color.

We spent extra time in Shakespeare's birthplace, where the Bard was born on April 23, 1564, and died on the same date fifty-two years later. The room in which he was born was furnished with the original bed, which was much shorter than modern-day beds. A small wooden cradle in which Shakespeare was rocked to sleep and a bureau completed the original furniture. A sign in the interior of the room read that 660,000 people pass through the house annually.

Strolling through the gardens of Anne Hathaway's Cottage brought back memories of other gardens we had visited the previous year in Europe.

"Isn't it remarkable how much attention goes into their gardens – everywhere in Europe," I commented.

"I was thinking the same thing, J.J. Remember Versailles?"

"Yeah, it was incredible," I said, thinking of the well-manicured, geometric-shaped shrubs, trees, and flower gardens. "And it's not just public gardens but also private ones. Remember the Dutch gardens in private homes? They were gorgeous – picture-perfect actually."

We meandered through the town square, popping in and out of shops, grabbing scones and teacakes at the various bakeries. The light frosting on top of the airy cakes gave them just enough sweetness to make them scrumptious, and

Dee – forgetting her diet – ate more than her share.

In Stratford, while sitting on a park bench eating our cakes and sipping on Pickwick tea, we met Lilly. She was probably in her 80s, and she huddled under her tiny umbrella as she watched her puppy – a bulldog mix – playing in the grass.

Prim and proper, her hair bleached to white with age, her demeanor screamed upper class without the snobbishness. Her perfectly ironed cotton navy suit and crisp white blouse seemed out of place among the vacationers, all in casual wear.

Lilly was a fascinating character. She had lived her life on the London stage during her younger years, retiring to Stratford to spend her days reading, tending her garden, strolling for hours with her dog – Jasper – and occasionally playing a bit part at the Royal Shakespeare Theatre, located on the edge of town.

Widowed for thirty years, her husband had owned a small clothing store off Regent Street in London. One night as she was performing at the Palace Theatre on London's West End, her husband and son were tragically killed in a fire. Their clothing store had burned to the ground. As her son and husband attempted to save the merchandise, the old building's timbers collapsed, trapping the two inside. Much of the block burned that night, killing three other people and injuring dozens.

Despite the tragic deaths of her family, Lilly had a wonderful outlook on life. She continued in the theatre for another twenty years before coming to Stratford to seek a more peaceful, restful life in her old age.

"Girls," Lilly said as she twirled her blue and white polka-dotted umbrella, shading her from the warm English sun," get out of life everything you can." She looked at the both of us, her eyes shining, "Life is truly a theatrical stage with surprises happening all the time. Don't waste a minute feeling sorry for yourself or crying about any woes that have been dished out to you. Give your best performance everyday – as long as God gives you breath – and smile all the while."

Dee and I talked about Lilly many times in the years to come when we had problems that seemed overwhelming. We remembered that day in the park with Lilly who had had tragedy in her life and yet had overcome it, focusing on the stars.

Sadly, at 4:30 we had to bid Lilly farewell as we headed for the bus going to London. When it arrived, we literally sank into the seats, exhausted. Immediately, I started looking through the small purchases I had made – postcards, a small statue of William Shakespeare, and a souvenir book on Stratford-Upon-Avon.

"This was really an exciting day, Dee. And tomorrow is Canterbury Cathedral." Getting no response from Dee, I glanced her way. Her eyes were closed with her head resting on the window. She slept all the way to London.

* * * * * * * * * * *

Canterbury definitely highlighted our time in England. During the twelfth century, the church was the focal point of religious pilgrimages from all over England, including Chaucer's famous pilgrims, who told their tales on the way to the Cathedral.

As we strolled through the church, Dee was awestruck.

"These stained glass windows are spectacular," she remarked, attempting to survey each window, which depicted Saint Thomas a Becket's life. "And look at the ceiling. I've never seen any ceiling with such a high arch. It's incredible," she concluded.

We walked between the immense columns within the church. The relief sculpture on the white, marble columns and around the massive doors to the church depicted biblical history and church doctrines. Rich and symmetrically-

43

carved, the columns were decorated in some of the most fanciful and bizarre patterns depicting imaginary animals. The Gothic-style ceiling of the cathedral seemed to soar with new freedom from that era. Huge amounts of space were given to windows of extraordinary height and color, and I craned my neck to get a glimpse if each varied sector of the casements.

It was perfectly silent in the chamber at that moment, and I touched Dee's sleeve so as not to break the quietude. "Unbelievable," I mouthed.

"I'm speechless," she replied, in a quiet, breathless whisper, as she stared at the spectacular interior.

Strolling through one of the many smaller chambers, we stopped to read some of the historical facts about the cathedral. The foundation of the splendid church dated back to Augustine from Rome in A.D. 597. Parts of the cathedral were destroyed in the 1174 fire, only four years after the murder of St. Thomas a Becket on the dark evening of December 29, 1170.

Wanting to learn more about St. Thomas a Becket, we followed signs to the site of his martyrdom. Apparently, St. Thomas served as arch-deacon of the diocese before he became archbishop. In 1170 – because he stoically defended the privileges of his office and his church – he experienced martyrdom in Canterbury Cathedral. He was slain by four knights of King Henry II, who was part of the increasingly sophisticated bureaucratic machinery and royal government of the age.

We stood before the altar of Saint Thomas a Becket – known as "the altar of the sword's point." Above it was a dark, bronze sculpture, representing the cross and two swords. The dramatic conflict and struggle between the universal church and the feudal monarchies of England were common at that time, obviously causing many unwarranted deaths.

We studied a series of stained glass windows, which

powerfully recreated parts of Saint Thomas a Becket's life. The bottom of the masterpiece was most interesting – the multi-colored glass depicted St. Thomas praying at the altar with three mailed knights beating on the cathedral door. Unbeknownst to St. Thomas, a monk and an armed knight were already inside the church ready to overtake him.

Sitting for half an hour, we listened to the choir practicing – the pure, soprano voices and organ music bounced off the massive walls, echoing throughout the sanctuary. It was as if every cubicle in the massive cathedral received the angelic sounds, held them, and then threw them back to us, resulting in the most glorious, resounding and reverberating echoes imaginable. The music literally engulfed us – it was bigger than life.

Several of the hymns we didn't recognize, but chills went up and down our spines as "The Lord's Prayer" concluded the choir's practice. It's difficult to explain the feeling of one's whole being coming together with God in Oneness, but that happened for me that day in Canterbury Cathedral.

Three hours was hardly enough to spend in the splendor of that spectacular, Gothic church. Finally, though, we pulled ourselves away and walked to the main gate through which the pilgrims had first entered the town hundreds of years before. There were still ancient shops at the entrance, selling potions, magic, and witchcraft.

"These were the stores that the pilgrims shopped for religious trinkets to bless and rid themselves of sin before they entered the church," I commented. "I read it in *Europe on Five Dollars a Day*," I added hastily as I noticed Dee's look of skepticism.

"What do you mean? Weren't they cleansed once they were in the church?" Dee questioned as she surveyed a window containing unusual relics that seemed to belong to twelfth-century England.

"Well, there were many villains who had money-making

ideas at that time, and they would convince the pilgrims that they needed additional help in order to gain God's forgiveness. These crooked shopkeepers then sold the innocent pilgrims many useless religious trinkets and relics."

"Really?" Dee glanced at me, interested.

"Yeah, and many of the clergymen were also scoundrels and made money off the uneducated, naïve church goers – the common people, you know – by selling them pardons. Apparently, crime has always existed," I added, staring at the various witchcraft items currently being sold from the store whose window display was our focal point.

"Is that what they call gargoyles?" Dee questioned, pointing at grotesque creatures cluttering a corner of one window.

"Oh, yeah. Let's go look," I answered, always fascinated by the half-human-half-animal features on the beast.

Apparently the shop owner was a bit obsessed with gargoyles as he relayed a multitude of details about them – more than we needed to know.

"The term gargoyle comes from the French word *gargouille*, meaning throat or gullet in English. Or other interpretations come from the Latin *gula* or *gar* meaning to swallow," he added.

"Oh," Dee muttered. "They swallowed humans?"

"Well, not exactly," the shopkeeper continued. "They were originally used as gutters which caught the water, throwing it off the roof of the buildings. So the throat and swallowing actually referred to water." He grinned as he continued. "However, in Rouen, France, a monster named *Gargouille* had appeared to the people. They sent an imprisoned, condemned man to capture him. That created a whole new legend." The man hesitated and then added, "And then at some time in history, gargoyles became monsters that actually scared off evil spirits so they were used for protection."

"Really?" Dee was even more interested now. "Protection, huh? I could get some of those little ones for my brothers and sisters. What do you think, J.J.? I was looking for new and different ideas for presents."

"Don't you think they're a little scary for the kids?" I questioned, picking up a black and gray hunched lion with the arms and hands of a human. "They wouldn't exactly fit in well with their Barbie and Ken collection."

"Oh," Dee replied. "Maybe you're right. Why don't you give me two of those green ones on the keychain. My two older brothers might like them. Cute, huh?" she asked, picking the little green ones up and turning them over in her hand to examine all sides.

"Not exactly the term that I had in mind."

At any rate, Dee had two gifts bought for two brothers. I was glad that she didn't have 13 gargoyles to stuff into her luggage. We continued to meander in and out of the shops, looking at all of the curious relics, often wondering about their meaning but were afraid to ask.

Amidst a light fog and drizzle – for which England was well known – we returned by bus to London in the late afternoon and decided that in the morning, we would take the ferry across the English Channel to Hoek van Holland, a Dutch seaport, and then catch the train north. By early evening, we would be in the charming Dutch city of Amsterdam.

"Should I phone ahead, Dee?" I questioned, mischievously.

"What are you talking about, J.J.? Phone where?"

"To the wooden shoe factory. We should make sure that they have a new supply of clogs for you to pack for your siblings," I smirked.

"Very funny, J.J. I could have bought those gargoyles for them and my shopping would have been done."

Yeah, that was my fear, I thought. A suitcase full of gargoyles!

"But I do have to find something different this year to

get for everyone," she said. Then as an afterthought, she added "but they did *love* their wooden shoes."

In Paris, we can check on berets with the kids' names embroidered on them," I noted, jokingly. "Or here's a unique idea – Swiss cowbells. It would help your mom keep track of the younger kids," I concluded.

"Actually, that's not a bad idea," Dee remarked, flashing me a smile. "We'll keep that one in mind."

"Well, we leave England tomorrow and head for the main continent. Who knows what adventures are in store for us there," I remarked sleepily with a yawn.

A truer statement could not have been made!

Chapter 5

The Staircase to Hell

We ferried across the English Channel. The ferry – so huge and foreign to both of us – seemed more like an ocean liner, and we loved every minute. Sitting outside in the deck chairs, the sea air was crisp and clean, and time seemed to stand still as we coasted over the sparkling, blue water and watched the azure sky, dotted with fluffy, white clouds. The large powder puffs changed continually, forming birds, butterflies, and even trains with billowing smokestacks. The sea gulls swooped and glided around us, diving for fish. As we sat above deck, the world became a combination of air, birds, sky, and water, and it was magnetic.

After two hours of fresh sea air, we decided to go below deck, stretching out in sleeper-like lounge chairs, and we snoozed the remainder of the trip, awakening as the ferry docked.

From the ferry, catching the train going from Hoek van Holland to Amsterdam was effortless. The train sat next to the ferry dock, awaiting any boarding passengers coming from England, and the only looming problem was getting our luggage up the three flights of stairs from the boat's storage area unto the waiting train.

Dragging and tugging the suitcases *up* the staircases was a tougher job than letting them slide down when we boarded. Some nice young man in a business suit standing next to us noticed our plight and offered a hand. Once aboard the train, we settled in some cushy seats and stretched out for our trek across "The Lowlands."

What a beautiful trip through the lush, green pastureland, spotted with cows, windmills, and fields of glorious flowers. Orange-tiled roofs topping red brick houses lined the canals and tiny, winding country roads. Picture-perfect flower gardens adorned each front yard, and white lace curtains showed at each window and door. Many windows were framed with half-curtains, allowing the potted plants to be displayed on the windowsills – yellow mums, purple hyacinths, and red geraniums lined the sills.

Looking at the multitude of windmills, I thought about a report I had done on Dutch windmills in high school social studies class, remembering that windmills came in various kinds and shapes, and each one had a different task to perform. One specifically-shaped windmill ground chocolate, another grain, and another dyes to be used on cloth. I knew that a knowledgeable person could tell its function just by looking at a windmill, but I didn't want to ponder any of that. I just wanted to sit and soak up the beauty of Holland.

Dee broke the silence. "You know, J.J., we didn't see any of this last year since we flew from London to Amsterdam. I really think the true flavor of Holland was lost since we saw only Amsterdam. This Dutch countryside is gorgeous," she concluded, her nose glued to the train window as we zipped over the flat land at 150 miles per hour.

It was late afternoon when our train arrived at the Central Station in Amsterdam. The VVV – the Dutch tourist agency – was situated in the train station, and the tall, friendly clerk found us a nearby hotel with a vacancy.

"Allow me to phone ahead to be certain of this vacancy," the Dutchman smiled.

"He is so cute," Dee whispered as we listened to him chatting on the phone in his guttural Dutch language.

"Yes, ladies," he said as he hung up. "A room at the Museum Hotel will be ready for you."

"Great. Do you have a map of Amsterdam?" I asked, knowing how confusing the hundreds of narrow canal streets could be.

"Yes, of course," he answered, grabbing a map from

under the counter. "The Central Station is here," he said, pointing to the map. "Just walk down Damrak, and the Museum Hotel is on the corner, right before the Dam. It's very easy to find," he grinned, handing us the map. "Okay," Dee responded, still not taking her eyes off the handsome, young blond. "Thank you so much. If we should get lost, we'll be back for more directions," she said as she cast one last look at him over her shoulder. Picking up our luggage, we started on our two-block trek.

Amsterdam was delightful because of the narrow, winding, cobblestone streets, flanked on both sides by three-hundred-year-old houses. Tall and skinny, the houses were all connected to each other, situated next to rings of canals. Previously, our first impression had been that they resembled gingerbread houses from storybooks. The houses – coupled with the circles of canals – created a quaint, picturesque scene of old-world Holland.

Dragging our bags through the street, which was crowded with tourists, we soon saw the hotel sign above the door of a beautifully gabled building, which was squashed between a restaurant and a souvenir shop.

"There it is, Dee. The Museum Hotel. That wasn't far."

"Gosh, I was sort of hoping to get lost to have another look at that Dutchman."

I ignored Dee's statement as I focused on dragging my luggage up the short flight of stairs leading to the outside door of the hotel. It was a small hotel but well maintained, as are most Dutch properties. Dark, flowered tapestry covered the heavy, oak couch and chairs, and paintings of Dutch landscapes spotted the walls. A middle-aged Dutchman in a gray sports jacket greeted us as we entered the hotel.

"Good afternoon, ladies."

"Hello. We've been sent from the VVV. Do you have a room available for us?"

"Yes, of course. Hans at the VVV said you'd be here in

about ten minutes," he replied, checking his watch. "You're right on time." He had a charming smile, which he flashed at us as he reached for a pen. "Please register here, and may I see your passports?"

While registering, I couldn't help noticing the staircase. We had experienced the small, winding Dutch staircases the previous year, but this one looked especially precarious. Actually, it looked like a god-awful nightmare. The ascension was at a ninety-degree angle and had a wicked S-curve.

As the clerk went to the back room to retrieve our key, I tapped Dee on the shoulder. "Hey, check out the stairs," I whispered. "No living being could get a suitcase up that spiraling, deadly entrapment. I wonder where the elevator is," I said, looking around.

"You are in Room 601, which is on the fifth floor," he said nonchalantly, as he returned with the key.

"Fifth floor?" Dee questioned. "Do you mean sixth floor?"

"No, Dee," I inserted, "remember that in Europe the floor numbers are different than in America. The main floor has rooms from 100-199 and the first floor has rooms from 200-299."

The hotel clerk nodded, "That's correct, miss."

"Oh, yeah, I forgot," Dee replied, "That's very confusing. So Room 601 is on the fifth floor."

Again, he nodded.

"And the stairway is behind you," he added, looking in the direction of the lethal stairs that I had just seen, "and the light switch is over there," he added, pointing in the same direction.

"Sir, excuse me," Dee added quickly. "There's no elevator? I mean, lift," she smiled.

"No, madame. Sorry."

We looked at each other in dismay and reached for our bags, which seemed to have grown to three times their size

52

as we thought about climbing to the fifth floor.

"Good grief, Dee!" I exclaimed when we were out of the clerk's earshot. "Five floors up that stairway to hell! It's bad enough that it goes straight up, but look at that corkscrew turn."

"Let's consider it a challenge, J.J. You know we were told last year that everything in Holland is small and narrow because they have run out of room in this tiny country. That stairway just fits."

Looking down at my luggage, I wondered how both the bags plus my body could possibly fit onto the stairs. I stood silently surveying the death trap ascending in front of us and decided to push the button for the lights, plunging headway into the seemingly impossible task.

About halfway up to the first floor, our uncontrollable laughter started. Maneuvering my two pieces of luggage on the S-curve – especially the fat, chubby neon one – was more than a challenge. It was a totally impossible feat.

"Dee, I'm stuck on the curve. Really, the luggage and I are too fat to fit through this twelve-inch space," I said in a fit of laughter. At that moment, I lost grip on my chartreuse one, and it tumbled to the edge of the bend in the stairway, landing upside down. After a struggle with the remaining suitcase versus gravity, I finally freed it from the hairpin turn when the lights went out.

"Oh, my gosh, J.J." Dee's voice came from somewhere in the dark. "The lights are out."

I realized that we had encountered European "timerlights," designed to click off automatically if guests forgot to turn them off – a clever European trick to conserve on electrical bills. Normally, there was plenty of time allowed to get from one level to the other but not with oversized luggage that had to be squeezed and tugged up a hopeless maze with a deadly hairpin curve in the center.

Sitting down as I started to laugh, I realized that my suitcase and I were not only stuck again on the next impossible curve, but now it was also pitch black.

"Okay, Dee," I said, finally getting control of myself. "Since you're ahead of me, set your luggage down and see if you can get to the first level and push the button for the light. We can't go any further in the dark."

Leaving her bags, Dee fumbled her way to the first floor and found the button. Stumbling, we now tried to drag, push, and tug our luggage to the next floor. But again laughter overtook us, and the lights went off before we completed our task. We sat on the steps and succumbed to our ridiculous situation. Five minutes later, we finally reached the first landing, sprawling on the floor in exhaustion and laughter.

"Dee, we've only gotten one-fifth of the way," I cried. "Who built his death trap and put hairpin curves on a stairway only wide enough for a stick-person? Even at full speed with no luggage, it would be impossible to climb this deadly maze and get to the first floor in less than five minutes." Dee was on the floor, rolling with laughter.

"Why not issue us a death sentence right now because we can't do this four more times," I said, looking up. Of course, we could only see as far as the next glaring S-curve and could only imagine the labyrinth of stairs that lay beyond.

Still laughing, I stumbled back down the stairs to retrieve my carry-on, lying uncomfortably upside down on one of the curves.

Somehow within the next twenty minutes, we managed to falter and flounder up four more flights of stairs amid the light-dark predicament of the timer-lights. Finally arriving on the fifth floor, we sat at the top of the stairs, still giggling and catching our breath. For a good five minutes, we sat and looked over the edge of the railing to view the deathtrap below. Finally, we gathered our bags, going in search of our room – Number 601.

"Here it is," Dee said as she fumbled for the key, which

she had tucked away in her pocket. She opened the door and turned on the light. Peeking in, we both stood and stared, speechless.

"This has to be a mistake," I finally uttered. "This must be someone's closet. At least, it's the size of *my* closet at home."

Two twin beds were pushed together. A sink was in the corner with a mirror hanging over it. That was it!

"Dee, I hate to mention this because it's a minor detail, but there's no room for our luggage in this room."

"It's a little small, I admit… " Dee started to say.

"That's an understatement of a lifetime," I interrupted, unable to believe this tiny space – encompassing the size of a prison cell – was really a room for which the hotel charged money. After the harrowing experience of climbing the five flights of stairs, we decided not to complain. A larger room might be another five flights up.

After a short discussion, we finally put our luggage on the two beds, unpacked our essentials, and then stacked the bags under the sink. Two people standing at once in the room was an impossible feat, so the major decision was who would use the sink first. If Dee used it, then I would have to stay on the bed.

Despite the dilemma, we sat – no laid – on the beds and laughed at the incredible and totally absurd situation.

Several years later when I moved to Holland to spend a few years abroad, I had many more experiences with lethal stairways. It was then that I learned of the poles with pulleys, which protruded from the gables at the front of the canal houses. These ingenious inventions made it possible to pull the furniture up through the windows. Stairways far too narrow to accommodate a dresser or couch were useless, but the pulleys made it possible to furnish an apartment with any desired furniture – even a piano that wouldn't fit into the narrow doorway of a canal building could be pulled through a large window three flights up.

The Dutch ingenuity outwitted the maze of staircases, which were even too small for a traveler and her neon carry-on.

After freshening up – one at a time at the sink – we grabbed our purses. Dee had discarded her red monstrosity for a smaller black one that she found at London's open market, and we exited our closet-sized room, closing the door on the entire predicament. We descended the stairs, which were still steep and winding but now appeared less lethal than they had when we ascended with luggage. We burst through the hotel doors onto the street, ready to stroll through the enchanting city of Amsterdam and soak up the ambiance of the evening.

Chapter 6

Awesome Amsterdam

Already in the heart of Amsterdam, we headed for Kalverstraat, a pedestrian street with no traffic. It meant "Calves Street" in Dutch, and in former days, the farmers would walk their calves through the street on their way to market. Today, however, as we walked slowly through the old street, we couldn't resist window shopping and observing the latest in Dutch fashions.

"Look at those wild platform shoes," Dee commented, pointing to red shoes with platforms heels at least four inches in height. " I should never have gotten rid of my red purse. It would have matched those shoes perfectly and would have been right in style in Amsterdam," she lamented.

"Yeah, well, your purse would never have made it up the stairs and certainly would never have fit into our room," I grinned. "Anyway, I'm sure we'll see many crazy sights now that we're in Amsterdam."

We strolled towards Leidseplein, a central area of outdoor cafés, and spent the next hour dining on the popular Dutch pea soup – *erwtensoep* – homemade bread, and dark, mocha Dutch coffee. Two bowls apiece of the thick, rich soup were all we could eat. However, by ordering something to drink after dinner, we were allowed to sit at the outdoor café and people-watch.

"Aren't the people of Amsterdam amazing!" I commented rhetorically after sitting in Leidseplein for nearly two hours. "Look at that wild-looking girl with blue and orange hair, wearing that leopard-skin mini-skirt and see-through blouse. Hey, look, she has on those platform shoes that we saw in the window," I laughed, "and right behind her is a couple in black evening wear, who are probably going to a classical concert."

I watched the couple as they strolled arm-in-arm past a canal house, and my eye caught sight of two homeless people huddled together in a small window well of that house. They were covered only with a thin, ragged blanket. Such diversity on the streets of Amsterdam, I thought. It was possible to see all classes of people in just one short evening at an outdoor café.

The street entertainers were extremely amusing, so we continued to sit and observe. A young French couple expertly coordinated a nearby puppet show, and on the other side of the square was a man on a unicycle, performing tricks. Adding to the amusement was a mime completely dressed in silver with a silver-painted face. He looked like the Tin Man from *The Wizard of Oz* and was an instant hit with the audience.

"Mimes always seem to be main attractions in all European cities. Have you noticed that, Dee?"

"Yeah, I have. It's probably because the crowd never knows what the mimes are going to do since they only move when they've received money from someone," Dee replied.

"This one is winning the hearts of the little girls," I noticed. "Look, he's kissing their hands after they put money into his hat there on the ground. Isn't it amazing how their movements are so smooth – almost robotic? It must take years of precise practice," I added.

"I read somewhere that mimes date back to the late 1800s, and being a mime is a true European form of art," Dee noted.

"Well, I'm going to get my hand kissed," I smiled, picking up coins from the table to deposit into his hat. "Take a picture," I added, slipping Dee my camera as I made my way toward the mime. Dee had forgotten her camera in the States, so we shared our one Kodak between us.

The Tin Man was standing perfectly still as I approached, and I casually dropped the coins into his hat. Instantly, he held out his hand. Glancing at Dee, I flashed her a broad smile and pointed to my camera sitting on the table. "Picture," I mouthed to her.

Holding my hand to be kissed, he took it and shook my hand rather than kissing it. Again, I glanced at Dee and grinned with a shrug of my shoulders, wondering what was next.

Starting to release my grip and walk away, I found that *his* grip tightened, and I couldn't move. There I was, still shaking hands! The crowd that had gathered started to laugh as they realized my predicament – I was trapped.

Hearing Dee's cackle in the background, I, too, started to giggle. Ten seconds later, we were still shaking hands and several flashes went off as pictures were being snapped with me in the grips of the Tin Man!

"Dee, help me out," I called as she maintained her distance, now snapping pictures and giggling.

Slowly, however, after about twenty seconds, a smile began to appear on the mime's face as he politely raised my hand to kiss it and then made a low, gracious bow. Instantly, he resumed his previous position of stoicism, standing perfectly still.

Now, being given my freedom, I smiled broadly at the Tin Man, blowing him a kiss as I returned to my seat.

Dee was still clamoring with laughter. "That was hilarious," she said between fits of giggles. "Got great pictures, too."

"Yeah, thanks for your help," I smiled, a twinge of sarcasm in my voice.

Dee returned a sheepish grin.

"Well, it was totally unexpected but admittedly quite funny," I continued. "His spontaneous reactions kept the crowd's attention."

A little girl with long blonde curls approached him,

dropping a few coins into the hat and getting her hand kissed. The grandmother escorted the child, and the little girl was obviously trying to persuade her to put coins into the hat, also. Rummaging through her coin purse again, the grandmother found some more change. Quite attractive and fashionably dressed in a chic black dress, the grandmother bent to put the coins into the hat when, surprisingly, the Tin Man switched his tactics. He slowly smiled, bowed to the lady, and bent down for her. He then pointed to his cheek.

"Hey, he wants her to kiss him on the cheek!" Dee noticed excitedly.

Again, the mime had the crowd's total attention.

The grandmother seemed game for anything as she grinned at her granddaughter, who was clapping and laughing. Rising onto her tip toes, the lady started to kiss the mime's cheek. As she did so, like lightning, the mime quickly and agilely turned his head so that the lady's lips missed his cheek and caught him on *his* lips.

The crowd let out a roar and spontaneously clapped as the lady – wildly surprised – bent over with laughter as well.

"That was great! He was so fast – and clever," I laughed, wishing I had been fast enough to snap that Kodak moment.

The mime now graciously bowed again to the grandmother and took her hand to kiss it.

"I could sit and watch mimes all evening," Dee commented. "They are so funny and entertaining."

We sat for another half an hour, people-watching and sipping our cokes.

As we sat in the ambiance of the Dutch evening, I began to silently reflect on our previous year's visit to Holland. Just one year before, Dee and I had arrived in Amsterdam, not knowing or understanding anything about Holland. In fact, when Amsterdam appeared as the final city on our itinerary, we weren't even sure in what country it was located.

"Holland – The Netherlands – are they the same country?" I had asked. "What language do they speak – German? Oh, Dutch. A tiny country like that has its own language?"

But once we arrived in Amsterdam, it was instant love. The city, with its thirteenth-century houses all lining the rings of canals, was nothing less than fascinating – it was old-world charm at its best. Hundreds of bridges spanned the canals. All were aglow with thousands of lights at night, creating spectacular affects for tourists enjoying a romantic evening on a canal boat.

More importantly, Amsterdam was unique among European cities because in a yet-conservative world in the early 1970s, surprisingly, almost anything was acceptable in Amsterdam – multi-colored hair, platform boots, six-inch mini skirts, skin-tight leather pants, and two-foot wide torn bellbottom jeans, all of which we had seen while sitting that evening watching the mime.

In the 70s, hippies from all over the world – playing guitars, singing, and smoking pot – covered the steps of the beautiful Dam Square in the center of the city. Vondel Park – once one of Amsterdam's most gorgeous recreational areas – had become another haven for the hippy population. Beer cans, empty cigarette packs, wrappers, and dirty knapsacks made the park into a littered wasteland.

We found it amazing that a country so small could be so liberal in its views and forgiving of the multitude of "foreign" cultures, which had invaded them. Drugs and prostitution abounded everywhere so, naturally, liberal-thinking people wanted to live in Holland because they could express themselves with no legal boundaries. Somehow, the Dutch lived comfortably with almost every nationality, open-heartedly giving them refuge. I had to truly appreciate the Dutch for their ability to accept diversity.

During the previous year, we had stayed two nights with a Dutch family – technically in a bed-and-breakfast – and we had learned a great deal about home life in Holland. This year we were looking forward to learning even more about the Dutch – a wonderful, hearty nationality with a robust sense of humor and a genuine love of nature. They were true lovers of the water. Not only did the North Sea surround the country, but also hundreds of canals zigzagged throughout the land. The Dutch boated on the canals all summer and skated on them all winter.

Dee suddenly interrupted my reverie. "Hey, J.J., what do you say – let's go back to the hotel. It's been a long day."

"Oh, okay," I said, trying to pull myself back to reality. "But first there's a surprise I want to tell you," I said, gathering my thoughts concerning a topic about which I had not yet approached Dee.

"A surprise? Well, what is it?" Dee asked excitedly. "You know I can't stand it if you keep a secret from me."

"Remember last year – we visited Anne Frank's house?"

"Yeah, of course," Dee answered. "It was a highlight."

"I picked up a book there," I continued, "that was written by Miep Gies, the lady that worked for Otto Frank. She provided food for the family while they were in hiding."

"Yeah, I remember you did." Dee looked at me anxiously. "Well, go on," she urged impatiently.

"I did some research and finally got Miep Gies' address last year. I wrote to her and told her how meaningful her book was to me, especially since I teach *The Diary of Anne Frank.*"

"Come on, J.J. Get to the point." Dee was getting agitated.

"Well, to make a long story short, we're going to get to meet Miep."

"What? You're kidding, of course!" Dee exclaimed,

unable to contain her excitement.

"No, I'm serious. When I wrote to her, I told her that I wanted to return to Amsterdam someday, and she wrote back saying that if and when I got to Amsterdam, I should go to her publisher and set up a meeting with her. I never told you about all of this because, of course, we didn't know we were returning to Amsterdam this year. Then once we made the decision, I kept it as a surprise, knowing you'd never quit talking about it once you were told," I said, smiling broadly.

"Oh, my gosh. We're going to meet Miep." Dee's brown eyes – twinkling with the prospect of such an opportunity – widened to the size of quarters. "That's so exciting. She's the only person still living that helped the Franks, isn't she?"

"Yeah." My enthusiasm was starting to build as well.

In the 1940s, Miep's work as a secretary in Otto Frank's spice factory gave her the opportunity to become a close family friend. When the Franks went into hiding, she was their sole source for supplying food. She had a special love for Anne, bringing her writing material and clothes as well as food. Miep's heart broke when the Franks were taken to a concentration camp, and she always maintained hope that fourteen-year-old Anne would return. Those hopes were dashed in 1945 when a letter arrived that Anne and her sister, Margot, had both died of typhus in Bergen-Belsen.

"I can't believe this. How were you able to keep this a secret from me?" Dee questioned with skepticism. "You have a pretty big mouth yourself, J.J."

"Well, admittedly it was a struggle to remain quiet, but once we made our decision to come to Europe…well, okay, *I* made that decision," I laughed. "Anyway, I just thought it would be fun to make it a really big surprise." I paused. "Now, you probably won't sleep tonight, will you?"

"Well, I probably won't because now I have to figure

out what to wear when I meet Miep Gies," Dee replied with a wry grin. "If only I had known, I'd have packed something special," she lamented, a twinkle in her eye.

Silently, I hoped that her red, white, and blue sailor top was dirty.

"We can always go back and buy those red platform shoes. They would make a lasting impression on Miep," I replied, my usual sarcasm showing.

Dee threw me a snide grin as she began her nonstop babbling all the way back to the hotel.

After we climbed the stairway-to-hell – much easier this time without luggage – and entered our pocket-sized room, I tugged first my brown and then my chartreuse suitcase from under the sink. Rummaging through my carry-on, I finally retrieved Miep's letter. Presenting it to Dee, I watched her read it in awe.

Parts of the letter she read silently, but sections she blurted out in excitement. She read several parts of the letter, enunciating specific words and phrases as if I had never seen the letter at all.

"'My husband and I must visit many countries where our book is coming out because people want to see us and know that we really exist.' Imagine that, J.J." Dee exclaimed. "They travel all over Europe to meet people, and yet they want to meet *us*."

I nodded in recognition.

"Oh, listen to this. 'When you come to Amsterdam, stop by my publisher's office. He will call me, and then I will see what I can do for you.'"

Dee looked at me wide-eyed. "Oh, gosh," she said when she finished the letter. "Do you know where this publishing company is located?"

"Yeah, I found it on the map. It's close to our hotel," I answered. "We'll go early tomorrow morning to see if arrangements can be made for an afternoon meeting."

"Wow! Let's get some sleep so there are no bags under

my eyes when I meet Miep. This is the most exciting thing that has ever happened to me. I'm sure glad you have a camera."

Dee was talking in her usual rapid, stream-of-consciousness speech, hyperventilating with the mere thought of the adventure.

"You'll have to take a picture of Miep and me so I can have thirteen prints made for my brothers and sisters. This will be an even better present than last year's wooden shoes – and a heck of a lot lighter."

Chapter 7

Meeting Miep

Getting up early the next morning, we dressed and ate a hasty breakfast of fruit, yogurt, hot chocolate, and Holland rusk, topped with rich, yellow Dutch cheese. Checking the map again for exact directions, we jaunted to the publishing company, located on Prinsengracht, just a short distance from our hotel.

Looking at the street numbers, the old thirteenth-century canal houses all looked like someone's home. However, my trusty guidebook had told me that all of the old houses in the inner city were actually office buildings, hotels, or factory warehouses. We double checked the address and mounted the outside stairs. There, on the inside office was the name "Simon and Schuster, Netherlands' Branch" printed in bold letters on the door.

"*Goeden morgen, mevrouw. Kan Ik U helpen?*" a young lady in a blue and white flowered dress asked politely. Her long honey blonde hair was pulled neatly into a ponytail.

"Good morning," I answered quickly in English.

"Oh, good morning," she automatically switched to English. "May I help you?"

"We're hoping to meet Miep Gies. I have a letter from her." Proudly, I presented the letter, feeling important to have a personal letter from Miep Gies.

The young lady glanced quickly over the letter. "I'm so sorry, but Miep is elderly and doesn't entertain visitors anymore."

"But you don't understand," I interrupted. "As you see, this letter states that she will see me. My friend and I are very interested in Anne Frank, and, in fact, in America I teach *The Diary of Anne Frank.*"

I flashed her a smile, satisfied that this tidbit of information would gain an apology from Simon and Schuster's employee and that our meeting with Miep would be clinched. However, the young lady continued to insist that Miep's health didn't allow her to have many visitors. With a solemn promise to keep the visit short, I continued to plead. Obviously, I was testing the young lady's patience. I'm sure she must have been thinking "pushy American," but she remained polite.

"I'm sorry, miss," she continued to glance at me, "but..."

"Please, it's so important. You see my grandmother loved the story of Anne Frank, and she is dying. Her last statement when I left America was to be sure to see the lady who saved Anne." Tears welled in my eyes as I choked out the last statement.

The young lady let out a sigh. "Well, if it will make you feel better, I'll call her. I hate to disappoint your grandmother. But I must tell you that Miep hasn't seen any visitors in weeks. Wait here, please."

As the young lady exited into an adjacent room, Dee threw me a dubious look and whispered, "J.J., what do you mean that your grandmother is dying?"

"Well, okay, she's been dead for three years, but she did always like the story of Anne Frank. That part was true," I concluded, a bit embarrassed.

"It was a great try, but we're not going to get to see Miep," Dee said, sporting a hound dog look. "God doesn't like liars. It says that somewhere in the Bible," she concluded.

Not affected by her comment, I responded, "Don't give up yet, Dee. The young lady is making a phone call."

"Yeah, she is, but you know..."

Dee's sentence was interrupted by a squeal coming from the adjoining room.

"I wonder what that means?" I questioned, looking curiously at the door to the room.

At that moment, the young lady burst in, her face beaming. "I don't know why, but Miep says she wants to meet with you!" The excitement in her voice was genuine. I looked at Dee whose eyes were the size of quarters, and I gave her a smug smile. Actually, no one was more surprised than I was, but I feigned confidence.

Our visit was set with Miep and her husband, John, for the following day, 11 o'clock in their apartment. The young lady reached for a small notebook and pen, scribbling Miep's address and directions and drawing a hasty map. Dee and I remained speechless, hardly able to believe our ears.

"I hope the address and directions are clear. Do you know where Vondel Park is?" she asked.

"Yes, I think so," I answered.

"Good. The map starts there," she commented, handing me the paper. "Please, keep your visit to half an hour."

"Oh, thank you so much," I remarked, seizing the paper. I really wanted to kiss her, but I settled for a handshake. Barely able to contain my excitement, I glanced at Dee whose entire face was plastered from one end to the other with a smile.

Retreating to the street, Dee and I both let out a "whoop" that was heard in the canal houses up and down Prinsengracht.

"You did it, J.J. Tomorrow morning we meet Miep."

"God, forgive me for that tiny, white lie. Gosh, I need to sit down a second," I inserted. "My knees are weak."

We sat on the steps of the canal house, reading the directions to Miep's house. We decided it shouldn't be difficult to find her apartment, catching Tram Number 4 from Vondel Park and changing to Tram Number 26 as we reached Cornelius Pieter Laan. Picking up a bouquet of flowers in the morning from one of the street vendors would be a priority since I had read in several guide books that visiting a Dutch person's house without taking flowers would be unthinkable.

"Now that we have the rest of the day free, let's go to the Rijksmuseum," I suggested. "Last year we had to rush through it, and this time I want to literally sit and feast my eyes on Rembrandt's *The Night Watch*. That is such an incredible masterpiece."

"Okay, I'm game."

We went first to the Rijksmuseum, and I sat on a bench near Rembrandt's most famous painting of the musketeers ready for battle. The dark, somber tones of the painting were highlighted with hues of yellow. The artwork spanned the length and height of the wall. Understandably, *The Night Watch* had long been considered the masterpiece of Dutch seventeenth-century art.

We spent several hours in the museum, attempting to soak up the beauty of the centuries-old artistic masterpieces. The time was insufficient, but we thought that maybe we could return the next day. Of course, with all of the sights available in Amsterdam, that didn't happen.

We then strolled through the open markets, purchasing fresh apples, bananas, and Dutch cheese from the food stalls. Some wonderful posters of Amsterdam aglow at night caught our eye, so we each bought several scenes, thinking they would look great in our classrooms. Having packed a poster tube before leaving the States, it was situated length-wise in my brown luggage. We spent an hour in the market, which was located on a narrow, picturesque, brick street alongside a canal. Because of our meeting with Miep, we decided to make a stop at the Anne Frank House to refresh our memories.

We stopped in front of 263 Prinsengracht, trying to imagine living in the Secret Annex – as it became known – in back of the spice factory, owned and managed by Otto Frank. For two years, the four attic rooms became home to eight Jews in hiding.

Walking behind the hidden bookcase and up the steep staircase to the attic, we entered the dark world of the 1940s and Jews in hiding. I tried to imagine how Anne must have felt to shut out the world for two years. The rooms were small – typically Dutch – with mattresses or cots in the bedrooms. The dining table, sink, and stove occupied the van Daan's bedroom with no space left unused. Still remaining were the movie star photographs that Anne had pasted on her bedroom wall but now were covered with glass to keep unwarranted fingers from picking off pieces for souvenirs.

Silence was predominant as people slowly walked through the Secret Annex, room by room, trying to remember some of the instances that they had read in *The Diary of Anne Frank.* Young and old alike stopped to gaze out the open window, looking onto the steeple of Westerkerk, the church that chimed every half hour and reminded Anne that there was another world besides the Secret Annex – one in which people walked free of the yellow stars. This open window had normally been covered with blackout paper, sealing the free outside world from those hidden inside.

Similar to the previous year, I breathed deeply of the outside air once we made the steep descent to the street, knowing that Anne's first breath of outside air after two years of confinement was when she was taken prisoner to Westerbork, Auschwitz, and finally Bergen-Belsen where she died two months before freedom reigned.

Hoping to lighten the evening, we concluded with a canal boat ride, which allowed us the spectacular views of the monuments, buildings, and cathedrals, all aglow with floodlights. The open-topped boat drifted lazily through the Amsterdam canals, which were adorned with bridges, all twinkling with millions of tiny lights. We caught a glimpse that night of that beautiful city, which we wanted to cement into our minds.

"And there to your left are seven bridges in a row – all

lit up for the evening," the canal boat tour guide said in Dutch, English, German, Spanish, French, and Italian.

"Snap a picture, quick, J.J. That is beautiful."

Sitting back down after capturing the moment, I remarked, "You know, it's incredible to me how these guides know six or seven languages and can just flip from one to another. Don't you find that remarkable?" I asked Dee as she peered through the window of the glass-topped boat, gawking at a nontraditional couple involved in an unusual public display of affection.

"Huh? Oh, yeah. J.J., look at those two men…"

The tour guide interrupted her sentence, focusing the crowd on the oldest church in Amsterdam.

* * * * * * * * * *

Just as we exited the boat, Dee caught sight of a familiar face.

"J.J., there's that hunk we saw at the VVV the day we came into Amsterdam."

"Are you sure?" I questioned, not as infatuated with him as Dee had been.

"I'm positive," she replied, pushing ahead to catch up with him. "Hey, hi," Dee said, tapping the young man on the shoulder. He looked puzzled as he tried to place Dee's face.

"You found us a room at the Museum Hotel the other day," Dee quickly commented with a smile.

"Oh, yes, of course," he answered as he seemed to recognize Dee. "I see you're enjoying the sites of Amsterdam," he grinned.

Having just gotten off work, Hans van Huisen had taken the opportunity of seeing Amsterdam on a beautiful starlit night, and I wondered how I hadn't noticed his handsome, suave demeanor when we first met him. He spoke with a slight accent, which only added to his charm. Inviting us to join him for coffee, we went to an outdoor café across from the boat dock.

Hans had led an interesting life. Having been a Dutch Marine for six years, he had lived all over the world, guarding the Dutch Embassies. The last assignment of his six-year duty had been in Washington, D.C. Hans had loved America and especially our nation's beautiful capital. The Dutch Embassy, tucked away in an exclusive area of the District of Columbia, housed the Dutch Ambassador and fifty Marines from Holland. He had had plenty of free days while in D.C. and took advantage of visiting the White House, the Smithsonian, The U.S. Senate and Congress, Mount Vernon, Gettysburg, and, of course, the incredible D.C. zoo, secretly nestled in the midst of the busy city.

Having lived in fascinating cities around the world, he returned home to settle in Amsterdam. "I guess my heart is here," Hans said as we questioned his decision. "I traveled the world in search of myself but found that all the time I belonged in Amsterdam. I can visit all of those other places on holiday, but here is where my heart is. My parents, brothers, and sisters are all in Holland, and family is very important to me."

We left Hans that evening feeling a little homesick for our own families so far away in Illinois. We didn't want to go home yet because there was still so much to see, but we missed America and our loved ones. In the next day or so, a quick phone call home relieved our temporary homesickness.

In years to come when I was living abroad – being driven there by the restless spirit to travel and find myself – I thought of that night with Hans. Many times I was homesick for my homeland and my parents, but I knew I still had unanswered questions about life and what I was trying to attain from it. However, I felt certain that in the end – like Hans – I'd return home. It was where my heart was and where my family had roots.

* * * * * * * * * * * * *

Returning to our hotel by 11 o'clock, we snuggled into our tight, cozy room and talked late into the night, preparing questions and bits of conversation for the next morning's visit.

Checking her watch, Dee suddenly said, "J.J., it's 1:30, and I just remembered that I don't want bags under my eyes for my photograph with Miep. I've got to get my beauty rest," she concluded in her dry sense of humor. Hastily, she flipped off the light switch on the wall, less than an arm's length away.

"Gosh, Dee, I'm all fired up with thoughts about tomorrow, and now suddenly you want to sleep."

"Have to look my best, J.J. This is going to be a Kodak moment that will never be repeated."

"Well, okay, I guess I'll try to sleep. The alarm is set for 8 o'clock. That should be plenty of time to eat, dress, and find Miep's apartment building," I added.

Actually, it was a restless night for both of us due to the anticipation of our meeting. Finally, by 8 o'clock – having just fallen into a deep sleep – I was awakened by the uninviting sound of the alarm.

Showering and dressing in precision time and gulping our continental breakfast, we grabbed our map and purses.

"What are you looking for, J.J.? Let's go," Dee chided as I lagged behind.

"I can't find my camera." I felt panic setting in. The proverbial lump in my throat was eminent.

"You had it last night on the canal boat. You took pictures."

"Yes, and I think that's exactly where it is now – on the boat."

"Good grief, J.J., you left your camera? It's going to be our one chance for a photograph with Miep."

"Dee, if we hurry, we can go to the boat harbor first;

74

with luck, someone from the excursion company may have found it." The lump in my throat was starting to grow, and swallowing didn't make it disappear.

"Well, come on. Let's hurry," Dee said, dashing from the room and blazing the trail down the corkscrew staircase.

We raced to the harbor where we had caught the boat the previous night, and a blonde-haired, rosy-cheeked man was just opening the ticket booth. "No, no one has turned in a camera, but you're welcome to search the boat yourselves" was his answer to our critical question.

Dee and I dashed onto the boat and went directly to the back where we sat. There, lodged between the seat and the inside panel of the boat was my camera. Breathing a long sigh of relief, we thanked the attendant, and I uttered an "I'm-sorry-God-about-yesterday's-little-lie-about-Grandma" prayer.

Holding my camera tightly, I jogged to catch up with Dee, who was scurrying to the nearby corner to check the tram schedule and map. Tram Number 81 would take us to Vondel Park, and from there we had directions for the rest of the way. We sank onto a bench to await the streetcar. Trams were frequent in Amsterdam, as they constituted one of the main means of travel. Within five minutes, Number 81 pulled up with a dinging of its bell.

Fortunately, the journey across town was easy and uneventful. I was still saying a string of "Thank-You-God" prayers as I thought of missing a picture of this memorable event.

"J.J., quit berating yourself. You got your camera," Dee finally said, hearing my continual one-way conversation with God.

"Yes, but we could have missed the one opportunity for a picture of Miep because I forgot my camera."

"Remember, I forgot to even *bring* my camera."

I nodded and sat back to watch the string of old-world

houses along the tram's route.

We bought flowers from the vendor near Miep's house – a flourish of yellow, red, and purple flowers were neatly bundled in cellophane. Dee proudly carried the fragrant bundle as we approached the apartment building at precisely 11 o'clock.

Meeting Miep and John Gies proved to be the highlight we had anticipated.

"Please, come in," Miep smiled. With the European greeting of a kiss on both cheeks, Miep bustled to the cabinet for a vase, and John escorted us to the living room. Miep, neatly dressed in a soft flowered blouse and navy skirt, looked exactly like the pictures I had seen of her. White hair cut short and perfectly coiffed gave her a younger-than-eighty-years-old look. She entered the living room with the bouquet, and with obvious pleasure, she placed the flowers in the center of the coffee table.

"They are beautiful. The Dutch love fresh flowers in the house all year long," she remarked with a rather thick accent, arranging them perfectly in the tall, Delft-blue vase. I wanted to examine the vase, but I knew I shouldn't without permission.

"That's a Delft-blue vase, isn't it?" I questioned, hoping to open the conversation.

"*Ja*, it is," Miep smiled. "It's traditional old-world Dutch pottery."

"We've seen it in all of the stores. Is the pottery all hand-painted?" I asked.

"*Ja*, the pottery is delicately painted by artists who originated in Delft, Holland, centuries ago. It's beautiful, don't you think?"

Seeing I was interested, Miep crossed the room to retrieve another smaller vase and a tiny porcelain shoe, all painted in the Delft-blue tradition. She handed them to us to examine.

"Just look at the tiny windmills and flowers. You have

to be a talented artist to paint this," I commented, intrigued at the precision of the artwork.

"You have to have a steady hand for sure," Miep laughed as I wondered how anyone had the patience or ability to paint such minute details.

John had exited to the kitchen to retrieve a tray full of Dutch cookies and a pot of fresh Dutch coffee. Miep poured demi-cups full of the aromatic brew for each of us and passed the cookies.

Nibbling on the cookies, our conversation gradually switched not only to the war, but also to Anne and her family's plight while in hiding. Miep described the difficulties in feeding the eight people in hiding, including the four Franks, the van Daan family of three, and Dr. Dussel. Possessing eight fake ration cards, Miep went from one store to another in search of enough food for the hidden Jews. Many butchers and grocers were empathetic to the Jews' plight and never asked questions. It was essential to search for merchants who shared this empathy.

Miep remembered one morning on her way to see Mijhneer Sampson, a butcher who had been selling meat to Jews in hiding. As the shop was just opening, Miep was shocked to see the German soldiers hauling the butcher into a patrol truck, which took people to a holding area and eventually to a concentration camp. Someone had obviously "ratted" that Mijhneer Sampson sold food to Jews in hiding, and the empathetic butcher would be punished the same as a Jew – imprisoned and possibly put to death. It was the last time that Miep saw the butcher. Such disappearances became customary in those dark days in Amsterdam.

When food ran low in the city, Miep was forced to ride her tireless bike into the countryside in search of vegetables, eggs, and milk. More than once she was nearly caught by Nazi patrols as she re-entered the city borders. Somehow, Miep felt, God protected her because there was no other explanation as to why the German soldiers didn't see the packages – consisting of milk, vegetables, and eggs – bulging from under her coat.

"I must tell you," Miep inserted during a break in our conversation, "that I didn't do anything special that hundreds of other good Dutch people didn't do, also."

"But it *was* special, Miep," I insisted.

"No, not really. There were so many Jews hiding in Amsterdam, and we Dutch just did what anyone would have done under the circumstances. We helped the Jews, and I truly didn't do anything out of the ordinary." I felt her humbleness as she uttered these words in true sincerity.

Going to a cabinet, Miep retrieved Mrs. van Daan's compact, Anne's yellow Jewish star taken from her outerwear, and her faded yellow and white combing shawl, which was used when Anne combed her hair. I especially remembered the combing shawl because I always found it unusual that someone would put something over her shoulders so as not to get hair on her clothes. I wanted to pick it up to examine it more closely, but I felt that I would be considered presumptuous, so I simply snapped a picture. As I visually examined the star more closely, I asked, "How do you pronounce J-o-o-d?"

"Yode," Miep replied.

"Well, I assume that *Jood* means Jew?" I asked, still scrutinizing the well-preserved yellow cloth star, which was lying on the table.

"*Ja*, all Jews, of course, had to wear their stars in public," Miep commented.

"You know," John, who had been quiet most of the time, interrupted, "The Dutch and Danish were the only ones that had enough courage to stand up to the Germans. The Dutch actually wore yellow tulips on their coat..."

John paused, pointing to his coat collar, fumbling for the word. I offered "lapel."

"*Ja*, thank you," he smiled. "Lapel to show their support to the Jews."

"I read that in Miep's book," I replied. "That was amazing. Did you wear a yellow tulip, John?"

"*Ja*, we both did – everyday," he answered with a proud smile.

We took pictures not only of all of the objects that Miep had so lovingly saved, but also of Miep and John, sitting on the couch, hand in hand.

Miep seemed to enjoy sharing these past memories with us, and soon she was telling us of her early childhood in Vienna, Austria, during WWI when her parents sent their starving eleven-year-old daughter to Holland. Hundreds of malnourished Austrian children were sent to Holland where things were better.

Miep's adopted family – the Nieuwenhuises – rescued her from her deprived physical state, restoring her health. Several years later when the war ended, Miep chose to stay with the Nieuwenhuises instead of returning to her native Vienna and her birth family. The love of the kind Dutch people had been instilled in her, and Holland became her permanent, beloved country. Our conversation and time spent with Miep and John Gies was so memorable, and before we knew it, we had stayed our half-an-hour limit.

Looking at my watch, I noted, "We really must be going, Dee."

I hated to pull myself away from this momentous meeting, but Dutch customs allowed only a short visit with strangers.

As we rose to leave, I took Miep's hand. "Thank you so much. This has been the highlight of my life – meeting you, Miep."

She corrected me, "No, this is just *one* highlight because your life will be filled with many."

We politely shook hands with John, too, as we said our final good-byes.

After descending the stairs and reaching the street, we looked back at the Gies' apartment window, and there they were – Miep and John – waving. We returned the wave as we headed for our tram stop. What an exciting half hour we had spent in the Gies' household – a memory that is still vividly alive for me today.

Chapter 8

Herring in Holland and Mark-Less in Germany

For a week we meandered over the back roads of Holland, visiting the countryside and the villages of Edam, Urk, Volendam, and Schagen that were centuries old. Landscape and lifestyle were so much different outside the bustling city of Amsterdam. It reminded me of going to small Midwestern towns located in the middle of the cornfields after being in Chicago.

"It's difficult to believe we're still in Holland," I remarked, strolling through the village Edam. "The slow pace is incredible after the rat-race speed of Amsterdam."

"Yeah and everything is so quaint," Dee noted as we looked at the age-old canals, flower boxes in the windows overflowing with colorful blooms, cobblestone streets, and orange tile-roofed houses. The village could have been straight off an old postcard or a seventeenth-century painting in the Rijksmuseum.

We stayed in the only hotel in Edam, one located over the village's tavern. Quaint was hardly the word to describe the inn. It was more like pre-World War I and antiquated. Surprisingly, there was running water in the room, but there was only one twin bed and a cot.

"Do you think that there is really a mattress on this bed?" Dee asked as she sat for a moment on the edge.

"Well, even a straw mattress would beat this cot," I said, eyeing the foldable contraption sitting in front of me. Actually, the floor was looking "soft" at this point, but I offered to take the cot, leaving Dee with the "fluffy-mattressed" bed.

Long into the night, we could hear the Dutchmen singing and laughing in the tavern below us. With not even a lock on the bedroom door, we really didn't fear anyone breaking into the room. We both had a feeling that no one had used the hotel in decades, and the men in the tavern wouldn't dream that there were guests above them.

We went to breakfast the next morning, wondering what we'd encounter. The room had been an "experience." What could they serve for breakfast in a tavern? Obviously, the owner/bartender/waiter/cook – he was all four rolled into one – had been busy long into the night, and early morning risings were not his forte. With few – or no – hotel guests, he didn't have an established breakfast menu. Always, breakfast is included in the price of a European hotel, so I wondered what he was going to "whip up" at the last moment that would be suitable to serve. I didn't have to wonder too long.

Coffee came first. Every Dutch male is trained early in life to make the wonderful, mocha-flavored Dutch brew. However, with only coffee cups on the table, we were a little concerned.

"You *do* think we're getting food, don't you?" Dee whispered after our coffee had been poured and the waiter disappeared.

"Hope so," I answered.

Soon he returned, now donned in a full-length white apron. He was exceedingly short, so the apron dragged the floor and flapped around his feet as he walked. Silently, I prayed that he didn't trip with the tray of dishes he was now carrying. I doubted that this was a duty that he performed daily, and I didn't feel confident that he had ample practice in the balancing act.

I craned my neck, trying to see what delicacies were in store for us on the plates poised above his head. Even after the food was at eye level, I still wasn't certain exactly what it was, and I threw Dee a sideways glance as she, too, stared at the array of food that was being placed in front of us. The waiter disappeared, leaving us to ponder our morning meal.

I felt fortunate that I recognized one edible item – bread. It didn't look fresh, but I knew what it was. Everything else was a mystery. There was a dish of some kind of little sausages covered in what looked to be a sweet-sour sauce. Tasty for breakfast, I thought. Dee was ogling something unusual – pieces of mold is how I would have described them.

"Is that blue cheese, J.J.?" she inquired.

"Maybe," I remarked. "You try it and see."

A shake of the head told me that she wouldn't be the victim.

By then, a smell was permeating the air, and we knew it was coming from the third dish.

"What's that?" Dee asked, looking at thin slices of...of something. She bent for a closer look, immediately covering her nose.

"Fish," she cried.

"Ohhh," I remarked. "I've read in the guide books that the Dutch love smoked mackerel and raw eel. However, their very favorite is pickled herring with onions. I'll bet it's herring because those little slivers look like onions." I felt an inadvertent shiver go up my arms at the thought.

By then the waiter had reappeared, and I decided on a remedy to our precarious situation.

"Sir, do you have any eggs?"

"Eggs? Eggs? Oh, *eiren*. Yes, of course. How many?"

I looked at Dee who shook her head as she dived into the bread – her favorite staple besides pasta.

"Two, please," I answered.

Those were the days before anyone was well aware of the dangerous numbers of cholesterol, so I often started my day with two hard boiled eggs. Not a fan of fried eggs because of my sensitive stomach, it wasn't until the waiter left that a thought occurred to me.

"Dee, you *do* think the eggs will be hard boiled, don't you?"

"Well, probably. Maybe you should ask…"

The waiter/cook must have had the grease hot for *something* because it was already too late to ponder the question. Immediately from the kitchen came an unwelcome sound – crack, splat, sizzle.

"I'd say that they're fried," Dee said offhandedly.

Puffs of smoke – which soon grew into a solid haze – were already streaming from the area called the kitchen.

"Geeze, not just fried but rather scorched," I cried.

Dee was already doubled over with laughter, as I stifled a smile, trying to imagine what my upcoming breakfast would resemble. It was several minutes before I saw the results. Two tiny mounds of charcoaled blobs swimming in a small pool of grease arrived at our table and were placed in front of me.

"Anything else?" the smiling waiter/cook asked.

"Oh, no, thanks," I answered graciously.

Temporarily, Dee had repressed her laughter until he was out of earshot when she again burst into giggles.

"Are you going to eat that?" she asked.

"No, my stomach rebels just at the sight of a fried egg. Of course, these don't resemble fried eggs, but the puddle of grease is a sure sign that whatever they are have been fried. Do you want them?"

"No, I'm happy with the bread and butter."

"Well, save some for me," I begged, noticing that she had three slices buttered and stacked on her plate.

"Maybe we can get more," she suggested. "Even though it's stale, I know for sure that it's bread, which is really all that counts this morning."

After asking for more bread, I tried to move the "eggs" around on the plate so that it looked as if I had eaten some. Neither of us had the courage to try the "cheese" or whatever it was, and Dee covered the herring and onions with a napkin. We finished several cups of coffee along with all of the bread and quickly retreated to our rooms to gather our belongings. We left Edam with a new appreciation for comfortable bed, quiet room, and edible breakfast.

Journeying on to Volendam, I found that that charming village was my favorite. Dee took my picture with a fisherman, who had just returned with his morning catch. He seemed pleased to have his photo taken with me as he proudly posed with his fishing gear and string of fish. I stood on the old wooden boat with him, gazing at the nets, lines, and long wooden table to clean and cut the fish. The scene looked like something out of the past – tools and techniques of his ancestors. The fisherman wore his black, baggy pants, kerchief round his neck, flat cap, and, of course, wooden clogs. As I stepped off the old fishing boat, his wife – donned in a long skirt, apron, lace hat, and wooden shoes – arrived to help clean the catch of the day.

It was in Volendam that I bought a souvenir T-shirt. The front of the shirt depicted a man struggling to stay on his beat-up, flat-tired, black bicycle as he rode through the narrow, canal streets of Amsterdam. Surrounding him was the chaotic traffic of buses, cars, and taxis, with Tram #55 hot on his heels and about to overtake him. A Heineken sign loomed in the background, and a look of horror was plastered over his entire face. The caption read, "I Visited Amsterdam and Survived It."

I thought the T-shirt was cute because it reminded me so much of what it felt like to experience the craziness of downtown Amsterdam. At the time, I had no clue that it would express my feelings *exactly* at the end of nine weeks of incredible European adventures.

Volendam allowed us the opportunity to rent bicycles and venture out onto a dike, surrounded by water. The North Sea engulfed the dike on both sides, and we dodged the sea gulls that squawked their displeasure at our intrusion into their territory. It was a spectacular sight – the glistening water rippling with white caps was a showplace for dozens of sailboats, which glided over the glassy surface.

We pedaled for an hour over the dike and through the town – past sixteenth-century houses built on stilts to remain protected from the harsh North Sea storms. It was an afternoon of fun, sea, and wind as we bicycled through the streets and back alleys of Volendam, soaking up the ambiance of off-the-beaten-track Holland.

Eventually, we returned to Amsterdam to catch a train bound for Germany. Cologne was our destination. Spending time to buy food at the train station left no time to exchange money into German marks.

"We'll exchange our money once in Germany," I suggested. "As long as we have food to eat on the train, then we're all set. My stomach is the most important thing, you know." The green sides of my already chubby carry-on now bulged with two bottles of grape juice, an apple, two bananas, a container of yogurt, and smoked codfish.

* * * * * * * * *

The rolling, German countryside was beautiful, dotted with castles and fortresses on every plateau and hill.

"Look at those fortresses," Dee commented. "I teach about European history in social studies class, and we read about the hilltop forts, which were the Germans' means of protection from intruders on the rivers. When you look out the train window, don't you think you're reliving the medieval days?"

"Yeah, definitely. You know what fascinates me are the comforters, sheets, and pillows hanging out of each bedroom window," I said, my eyes following a row of houses in the distance. "The women must air them each day. That really helps me understand the compulsive cleaning techniques of my German mother – clean, clean, and then clean again. It all makes sense now," I smiled.

Growing up, I learned from my mother "you work first and then play." With this concept instilled in me early in life, it helped explain my workaholic-need to fulfill my daily routines before enjoying myself. Perfectionism ran a close second, often driving me into a tizzy to get everything done as perfectly as possible. The one trait I refused to acquire from my mother was the fanatic cleaning techniques that drove her to scrub, wash, and vacuum to excess. I could live with a little dirt in the house but not with any other kind of project done less-than-perfectly.

At any rate, my mother's fetish for cleanliness was all falling into place as I imagined that part of each German housewife's daily chores was airing the bed coverings, mopping her kitchen, and running the vacuum through the house. Such were my mother's routine duties each day. Incredibly, as we zipped over the German countryside, I noticed that even the landscape was spotlessly clean and impeccable. Unbelievable, I thought. These Germans keep the outside as clean as the inside.

Arriving in Cologne in the afternoon, we first checked the listing of nearby hotels, their prices, and available accommodations. We found the name of a nearby hotel, and then we looked for the window to exchange money. To our surprise, it was closed with a sign written in German.

"Well, all the banks should be open because today is Tuesday. Banks are only closed on Monday mornings, so it shouldn't be a problem," I concluded. "Let's walk to the hotel and look for a bank later."

Our plan was to spend one night in Cologne – long enough to see the magnificent cathedral and then move on to Heidelberg.

Walking to the hotel, Dee noticed something unusual. "J.J., look – the stores are closed. Germans don't take extended lunch hours like the Spanish. I wonder what's up?"

"I don't know. There's our hotel, though. Maybe we can ask the clerk," I suggested.

The small man with a mustache and pipe spoke enough English to get by – yes, he had a room for us; no, he wouldn't take American money; no, he couldn't exchange our money into German marks; no, the banks weren't open today!

"Sir, what do you mean the banks aren't open?"

"German national holiday. Everything ist shut. De banks open tomorrow at noon," he replied with a heavy accent.

We knew we were in trouble. In the '70s, credit cards weren't readily acceptable, and I had doubts that this German gentleman – born pre-war – trusted plastic. Immediately, he shook his head when I pulled out my Visa. Dejectedly, we picked up our bags and walked from the hotel.

"This is just great, Dee," I said sarcastically. "In London, we almost slept on the street because our hotel couldn't be located, and now we may be sleeping on the street because we have no money to pay for one. Who invented a German holiday that's celebrated in the middle of a week anyway?" I asked sarcastically, again taking the situation all too seriously.

"Let's not panic. There are other hotels on this street," Dee remarked, almost light-heartedly.

I wondered how she could be so optimistic *all* of the time. Pollyanna, I was thinking, but privately I wished I could possess the same easy-going personality.

As we walked down the block towards several other hotels, my thoughts wandered back to a time in college when I was too sick with a cold to attend a required concert. Even then, Dee's advice was carefree.

"Don't worry about it, J.J. You're sick. What can the professor do?"

"Lower my grade, that's what!" I exclaimed, as I endured spasms of coughing.

"Probably only a few points," Dee was quick to point out. "Don't sweat it," she remarked, nonchalantly.

I wished I could feel that way, I thought at the time, berating myself for being too grade conscious. But here I was now, getting upset over a matter that would probably be resolved quickly. We have no German marks – big deal, I tried to convince myself.

However, none of the other hotels on the block wanted to accept a credit card. Hot, exhausted, frustrated, and hungry, we sat on a bench to think.

"There's the cathedral, J.J.," Dee commented, looking over her shoulder. "Maybe we could get a pew in there to sleep on. It would be cool, safe, and free." Dee giggled, and I mustered a feeble smile.

We had always stayed in small hotels or pensions because they were less expensive; however, Dee now suggested we try a larger hotel. It would cost more, but we decided it might be our only way of getting off the streets of Cologne for the night.

Hot and tired, we dragged our bags towards a larger hotel at the end of the block and noticed two porters standing at the front doors. Porters not only meant that the hotel was expensive, but it also indicated that we would need money for a tip. We hesitated, trying to decide our next move.

"Listen, you wait here with the luggage," Dee suggested, "and let me go in alone to check on the price. I'll also check if they'll take a credit card."

"Good thought, Dee," I applauded her. She smiled at her intuitive idea.

Minutes later, Dee reappeared. "Well, they take credit cards, and although it's three times the price we're used to paying, I think we should take it. This hotel may be our only chance."

"How much is it, Dee?"

"It's thirty-five dollars," Dee frowned, a hefty price for us in the '70s, "but I don't think we have a choice tonight."

"Well, okay," I replied with hesitation, not wishing to part with extra bucks. "But, hey, Sherlock Holmes – how do we get past the porters with no money for a tip?"

"When I was inside, I noticed a back door leading to the parking area. Let's walk back there and see if we can get in," Dee suggested.

We tugged our luggage to the back of the hotel, and walking ahead to check the door, I gave Dee the "thumbs up."

"It's open," I called softly.

I saw Dee mouth the word "Hurrah."

"And, Dee, there's an elevator. No death-trap staircase," I said as she neared the door.

We tried to look casual as we entered the rear door, dragging our stuffed suitcases.

A very serious-looking German lady took my credit card. She accepted it only after scrutinizing my passport and American driver's license. Glaring at me over the top of her glasses, she demanded one more form of picture identification. Mustering a feeble smile, I pulled out my school ID, handing it to her after she threw me another sharp look. Checking the signatures on all of the forms, she snapped my passport shut, jabbing it into my hand. The rest of my documents she left in a stack on the counter.

As she exited to get our room key, I whispered to Dee, "Imagine what Helga Von Sunshine would have done if we had wanted to spend a week and not just one night. If I had only known, I'd have brought my bank statements, letter of recommendation from my principal, and clearance from the FBI." One of my flaws was my sarcasm, which reared its ugly head as I oftentimes mixed it with humor. It was a trait that I legitimately inherited from my father, and this time I thought that it was warranted.

Dee was trying to control her snickering when the lady returned with our key. I saw her throw my neon luggage a sideways glance, but resisted any change in facial expression. Picking up my ID's, I stuffed them into my purse and quickly headed for the elevator. We had now successfully passed the test with the hotel clerk plus we had secretly passed the porters without tipping.

Our room was beautiful and spacious. Lace curtains covering large French windows opened into a room filled with springy, soft sofas and chairs, plus billowy, down-comforted beds. A chandelier dripping with tear-shaped crystals was reflected in the large mirror, which was situated above the dresser. We were used to X-rated rooms in comparison to this luxurious penthouse.

We decided not to feel guilty about spending extra money that night because it was either that room or sleep with the homeless. Without unpacking, we went in search of food.

"This is ridiculous, Dee," I said after we had walked several blocks with no success of finding so much as a snack shop open. "What's a starving person to do even if he *did* possess German marks? Does everyone fast on this national holiday? And just where are the people anyway? If it's a German holiday, shouldn't they be celebrating with free brats and beer?"

Just then we turned a corner and a beaming smile greeted us.

"Excuse me, but I heard you talking. Are you Americans?" the young lady inquired.

"Yes, we are," I said, wanting to add that we were also tired, hungry, and "mark-less."

"I'm a Mormon from Utah. I'm in Germany extending the Word of God. Are you both Christians?" she asked, still smiling and graciously extending her hand to us.

Shaking her hand warmly, Dee answered, "Yes, we are Christians. Actually, we're American teachers traveling in Europe, and, at the moment, we're in search of food since all restaurants seem to be closed. Oh, did I mention that we have no marks either because the banks are closed?" Dee attempted to force a slight grin, and for the first time, I thought that maybe she was seeing the darker side of the picture.

"Yes, I know," the young Mormon replied. "It's one of those many holidays that the Germans celebrate. Actually, though, I can help you. There's a McDonalds a block from here, and they'll take American money."

"Really? Are you serious?" I asked, a bit skeptically.

"Yes, really. I'm headed that way so I'll show you," she replied.

We learned that her name was Sarah Connover. She and ten other Mormons had been sponsored by the Latter Day Saints to come to Europe to spread "The Good News." Dressed in a gray skirt and blue blouse, Sarah was not only attractive but also personable. Her long brown hair was pulled tightly into a ponytail, accentuating her high cheekbones, and she reminded me a little of Audrey Hepburn. We liked her instantly and by the time we reached McDonalds, we invited her to join us.

Staying in youth hostels, the eleven girls had started in Austria and were traveling by train across Europe, ending in London by mid-August. With only backpacks to carry their belongings, they received pamphlets and Bibles from Utah at designated American Embassies across the continent. From Cologne, they were going to Amsterdam and then up into the Scandinavian countries before ferrying across to England.

Brave and relentless in their missionary work, I found myself envious of Sarah and her task to which she was totally devoted. She and her friends had come to Europe with a single goal in mind – speaking to people about Jesus Christ. Taking no time for sightseeing, the eleven girls found complete pleasure in talking to people on the streets about God as well as speaking to small groups at churches.

Both Dee and I found it amusing that we had come 3,000 miles to have a lovely, young Mormon girl, who not only directed us to a McDonalds that took American money, but also made both of us ponder two questions. What do we want out of life? What is God's purpose for us? Sarah seemed so confident and sure of herself, and I longed for that same self-assurance.

It would be years before I matured enough to know exactly what I wanted to achieve, but this trip would bring me closer. At that moment, I knew that I had a restless longing to see more of the world, learn of other cultures, and be with people of different societies. Eventually, within the next few years, I would attain the experiences for which I yearned and would also draw closer to knowing who I was and what my purpose in life would include. Sarah – although about my age – was definitely ahead of the game.

That evening we three ate our dinner – consisting of cheeseburgers, French fries, and milk shakes – at the McDonalds that graciously took our American dollars. We spent an hour talking with Sarah as we exchanged adventures that we had had abroad. As we parted, we hugged like lifelong friends and wrote our U.S. addresses on McDonalds napkins in hopes of meeting again someday.

Because our real reason for going to Cologne was to see the fantastic cathedral, we decided to do that on our way back to the hotel. The immense structure housed the relics of the three magi transferred there from Milan, Italy. Considering the construction had been created in the 1200s, the Germans seemed to have excelled in building the twin picturesque spires – each 515 feet in height.

The enormous church was refreshing and cool. Again, the Gothic architecture contributed to the immense amount of horizontal space in the sanctuary. The interior was equal to 650 typical-sized American homes, and a ten-story building could stand on the cathedral's floor and not touch the ceiling. We felt like microcosmic creatures in a macrocosmic world.

While Allied bombers destroyed most of the city of Cologne during WWII, the great cathedral survived the war relatively unscathed. One story is that the Allies used the immense cathedral as a landmark to help them find their way to more strategic targets. Another story is that Allies couldn't bring themselves to destroy such a magnificent structure.

As we attempted to focus on the staggering size of the interior, the room was suddenly filled with the glorious sound of pure, angelic children's voices. We sank into the nearest pew to listen to the soprano sounds, echoing throughout the chamber in

A Cappella splendor. We were reminded of a similar experience a few days previous in Canterbury.

We could see the choir loft from where we sat, and even though we didn't understand the words, we recognized the tune.

"*How Great Thou Art,*" I whispered to Dee.

Glancing her way, I saw a tear trickle down her cheek. We spent the next half hour listening to the voices reverberating off the walls of the empty church.

The cathedral was, indeed, a masterpiece dedicated to the glory of God, but the children were God's masterpieces given to the congregation – and to us that night.

* * * * * * * * * *

We enjoyed our night of luxury at the hotel and arrived at breakfast early in anticipation of catching the 9 o'clock train to Heidelberg.

As we entered the breakfast room, our mouths watered. We had gotten used to the continental breakfast of rolls and coffee. This hotel's buffet – consisting of two tables loaded with food – was an exciting moment.

Mounds of fresh fruit – oranges, apples, kiwis, peaches, and grapes – covered one end of a table. A variety of breads and cereals completed that table, which was elegantly dressed in a white tablecloth with vases of fresh flowers. Cold cuts of ham, turkey, and beef along with cheeses, eggs, and yogurt were spread on another table.

94

Coffee, tea, and fruit juices finished the breakfast buffet.

I had already encountered the unfortunate experience with the fried eggs in Edam, Holland, but now I saw actual eggs still in their shells, and I was excited. Several times after Holland, I had ventured to ask for "hard boiled eggs" and had actually received them. I'd get two, sometimes packing one of them to eat later on the train. In my opinion, nothing could beat an egg for a mid-morning snack; in fact, a day without eggs was not complete.

At any rate, my eyes caught the sight of freshly boiled eggs next to the array of German cheeses. A kettle of boiling water next to the eggs confirmed the fact that they were freshly cooked. At least, that's what I *thought*.

"Dee, look at this. Eggs!" I exclaimed, returning to my seat with two of them nesting in egg cups.

I prepared the dark, German bread – still warm from the oven – with butter, which melted onto my fingers. Spoon in hand, I picked up my first egg and cracked it with a wallop. Dee's instantaneous laugh – along with my handful of raw egg – was my first clue that the boiling kettle of water placed next to the eggs was there for a specific purpose.

"Okay, what German joker would put raw eggs on the breakfast buffet for an unassuming, innocent – well, stupid – American like me?" I asked as I attempted to nonchalantly wipe my egg-covered hands with my small, dainty three-inch square napkin.

"Dee, help me out," I whispered. "See if you can find some more napkins, preferably larger and more substantial than this…this tissue." Dee was attempting to stifle her laughter when a few diners at the next table saw my predicament and grinned. I chuckled and shrugged my shoulders in an I-don't-know-what-to-do gesture. One tall German gentleman dressed in vacation wear chivalrously came to my rescue, offering me two large, cloth napkins.

"*Danke*," I said, using one of the two words I knew in German. *Auf Wiedersehen* – goodbye – was the other word

I knew, but I couldn't fit it into the conversation at the moment.

After cleaning up my mess and gaining control of myself – I, too, had had trouble stifling my laughter – I tried to act as if cooking my own eggs was an everyday experience. Confidently, I now walked to the bowl of raw eggs and took out two, carefully placing them into the kettle of hot water. Dee glanced at me over her shoulder as she ate her yogurt, obviously a safe selection on her part. In five minutes, my boiled eggs were done and ready to eat.

"Boy, the lessons you learn – boiling water at the buffet means I have to cook my own eggs. Maybe I should stick to safe food like cheese, bread, and juice."

Dee was still giggling as we went to our rooms to retrieve our luggage.

"Well, if we're lucky, we'll be in Heidelberg by this afternoon. My lesson has been learned, though, concerning raw eggs. No more surprises."

If only I had known that this was only the second of many "egg lessons" that I'd encounter in the following weeks. My adventure with eggs had only just begun.

Chapter 9

Eggs Became a Raw Topic

The train trip – which followed the Rhine River, eventually flowing into the Neckar River – allowed us the view of incredibly gorgeous scenery. Medieval castles fortified every hilltop, and farming terrain as well as green pastures and lush woodland covered the hillsides. I understood why my grandparents loved this land. Its spectacular scenery was straight out of an old-world postcard, I thought, as I feasted my eyes on the beauty of the rolling German countryside.

My thoughts drifted to my grandparents as I laid my head back and gazed through the train window. My maternal great-grandparents had lived south of Hanover on a farm until the 1850s. Years later, I would visit the lush, green hills that held the tiny village of Hummersen and become acquainted with my incredible Pollmann relatives, still living in one of the most beautiful areas of Germany. However, in the 1970s, I only knew that the Pollmanns had lived on a modest farm in the old Prussian section of Germany.

The train whistle let out a long screech as we neared Heidelberg, forcing me out of my reverie. We were cutting across the sunny Neckar River Valley and could see half a dozen church steeples towering over the maze of orange-tiled rooftops of the city.

We exited the train with our overly abundant luggage, and as we entered the main depot, I called to Dee who was charging ahead of me. Normally carefree and oblivious to the world, she acted as if she knew where she was going.

"Hey, Dee," I yelled, "*first* on our list is to exchange money. No more 'mark-less' days in Germany." I motioned toward the exchange counter at the far end of the station. "We're not likely to be lucky enough to run into another Mormon who will help us."

She smiled, nodded, and turned on her heel towards the exchange booth. We cashed enough travelers' checks for the next couple of days and turned to the hotel listings on the far end of the depot.

With a variety of hotels as well as pensions listed on the board, we decided on a pension because it was cheaper. In addition, it was located near the train station so we didn't have to lug our suitcases too far. By now, plump was a good word to describe Dee's luggage, which was growing by leaps and bounds as she added souvenirs for her siblings. Dolls in traditional Dutch costumes were perfect for a few of the tiny sisters while several wooden puzzles were purchased at one of London's open market for two of her brothers. Of course, there was the purchase of the gargoyle key chains from Canterbury. All of them were stuffed into her carry-on as she remained on a continual search for gifts for the rest of the family.

My bags, on the other hand, could be described as tubby, verging on rotund. Previously, they had looked as though they were full, but somehow they continued to expand. In addition, now and then I'd throw away empty containers of shampoo, hairspray, or toothpaste. I'd bought two or three of each, and as they were used, I'd toss them out, allowing a little more space in my luggage. Years later, I'd learn to bring mini-sizes so that I could throw them out more often, but in the '70s, I still brought large, economy sizes of everything.

I was stuffing inexpensive souvenirs into my bags to display in my classroom as well as traditional items to give to teachers and friends. Before too many more weeks, I would have to admit that I had been in denial concerning my obsessive buying of trinkets and that my chartreuse bag was truly no longer rotund but grossly obese. I was in trouble, and eventually I'd have to make a decision of either mailing a package of souvenirs home or buying another piece of luggage. Hardly able to tug the two grotesquely overweight bags through the streets of Europe, I knew that I couldn't handle a third. I had no choice – I'd have to spend money on a package sent home. At least I could choose ground mail (a slow boat) rather than airmail, which did save me money.

The pension that we chose turned out to be a huge, old mansion overlooking the beautiful Nectar River. We mounted the steep, cement stairs, leading to the outside door. Ringing the doorbell several times but receiving no answer, we slowly turned the door handle of the old, wooden door with beautiful, original stained glass border on both sides. It creaked, opening onto a dark flight of stairs.

"What do you think, Dee? Should we walk in?"

Hearing a noise far above us, we looked up the stairs, resembling something from a Frankenstein movie. They were gargantuan in width in comparison to the narrow, hairpin-curved staircase that we had maneuvered in Holland. These stairs looked like they belonged in an old medieval castle – one with no lights.

From above we heard, "Hello!"

"Hello," I answered. "Well, whoever it is, she knows one word of English," I smiled. "Obviously, they didn't have elevators when they built these castles, dungeons, or whatever this place is. My guess is that we'll have to walk."

Lugging our suitcases up four long flights of stairs, we plopped often on a step to rest. Finally at the top, we met the little, elderly lady who had yelled "hello." It truly *was* the only word of English she knew.

Somehow we communicated our need for a room – sign language works wonders when verbal language fails. She had a room for us with twin beds. Breakfast would be served on our balcony at 8 o'clock. All of this communication was done somehow with various hand signals, and afterwards we wondered how she had actually relayed this entire message so successfully

Instantly, we liked the short but round, white-haired Frau Hoffman. Attired in her tiny rose-printed housedress, her constant smile and giggles won us over. Her blue eyes sparkled as she straightened her tightly pinned bun on the nape of her neck. Once all of the rooming preliminaries were out of the way, we took our luggage to our small but comfortable bedroom.

"It's so cheery in here, and come look at this view, J.J.," Dee exclaimed. Pulling the sheer, white curtain aside, a tiny, private balcony was revealed overlooking the beautiful Neckar River. She opened the long French door, allowing us to step unto the balcony and breathe the fresh, clean air.

"This is a wonderful, old city," I commented, soaking up the ambiance of the romantic river scenery with old-world buildings following the bend.

"Yeah, it is. Let's go have a look," Dee said. "You know, we passed a café not far from here that was right on the river. Are you hungry?"

"Yeah, sorta," I remarked, grabbing my purse and camera as Dee picked up the key and pocketed it.

The small, corner café was a block away and overlooked the sparkling blue-green Neckar River. There was one outdoor table left next to the water, and an accordion player pumping out a German polka could be heard from somewhere inside the café. It was a perfect setting.

The menus were in German, and even with my German-English dictionary, we were not always successful with our translations. Looking around to see what people had on their plates was always the best way to decide what to order.

"J.J., make sure you don't order that thick cream soup which that lady just received. It has a raw egg floating on top."

I didn't know what fascination the Germans had with raw eggs, but I remembered that the previous year, a lot of German dishes had uncooked eggs floating on top. Looking at the steaming bowl of noodle soup that had just passed us, I didn't detect any raw eggs. My mind was made up – soup and sandwich.

"I'd really like some hot soup, but I'm not taking a chance. I'm getting a sandwich, salad, and yogurt," Dee concluded.

"We just saw a bowl of noodle soup, and it didn't have anything unusual on top of it. You need to walk on the wild side now and then, Dee," I said with a twinkle in my eye.

"Well, I know *exactly* what's in the yogurt, and I can see what's on the sandwich and salad. I don't know what's *in* the soup," Dee concluded.

"Don't be ridiculous. It will be perfectly safe."

We placed our orders, *somehow*. It's difficult to fathom now how we ever communicated our wants, but nonetheless we did.

Twenty minutes later my soup arrived, steaming and hot. "Dee, you should have gotten this. Smell it!"

"It smells great. Maybe I *should* have ordered some," she concluded.

It was delicious chicken noodle soup, just as my mother always made. Wide, juicy noodles in succulent chicken broth which I never could manage to master myself. There was always some ingredient that I just couldn't get exactly right, even when I followed my mother's recipe. Hers always tasted special. Anyway, it was my favorite soup, and I couldn't wait for a bite. Our sandwiches were fantastic – homemade dark rye bread with chicken, cheese, and tomatoes, mayonnaise oozing out on all sides.

While enjoying the food, Dee was chatting endlessly about the boats coasting down the river. Small sailboats as well as motorboats floated in harmony over the still, calm water, which reflected the sparkle of the afternoon sun.

101

"This is a fantastic city," Dee was saying. I was only listening with one ear as I suspiciously focused on my soup, and suddenly my spoon brought up something unusual from the bottom of my bowl.

"Oh, oh," I interrupted her as my hand stopped midway between the bowl and my mouth.

"What's wrong?" Dee asked, stifling a giggle in anticipation of something unwarranted.

"Apparently, the Germans have developed a new, sneaky, more improved technique in cooking – hide-the-raw-egg-at-the-bottom-of-the-bowl-of-soup."

Dee was already doubled over with laughter.

"When I get home, there's going to be some research done on this German raw-egg fetish. I'm beginning to think that those raw eggs at the breakfast buffet this morning actually were supposed to be eaten raw."

"Okay, J.J.," Dee said as she gained control of herself, "remember, this is a German custom. Now, don't make fun of it. This is all part of *your* German heritage."

"Easy for you to say – you don't have a raw egg floating anywhere in your yogurt." I stared at the egg, finally deciding to stir it into my soup.

"What are you doing?" Dee asked wide-eyed as she watched me.

"Mixing it up so I can't taste the raw egg," I answered, vigorously stirring. "No need wasting the soup. After all, it's paid for. Remind me, however, not to order chicken noodle soup again in Germany."

I thought for a moment and then added, "Maybe that special ingredient in my mother's soup was actually a raw egg, and I didn't know it." I pondered that thought and added, "Nah, I doubt it."

After lunch, we walked the pedestrian street in Heidelberg. The University of Heidelberg was located in the city and was Germany's oldest college, founded in 1386. It was located in a maze of dark alleyways with medieval fortress-like houses bedecked with brilliant flower gardens. From the university area, we walked to the Karl-Theodor Bridge. The ancient bridge, finished in 1758, sported a spectacular arched gateway across the Neckar River. Two towers flanked each side of the bridge – one was comprised of dungeon cells while both were part of the medieval fortification of the town.

From the bridge, we strolled to *Kornmarkt* – the center of the old city – and from there, we took a cable car to the castle, which rewarded the observers with a great view of the city. The cable car stopped in front of the castle's wall, which was in ruins with many of the stones tumbled by erosion or destroyed in medieval battles. The crumbling façade was a true testament to the ancient structure surrounding the castle – all dating to the fifteenth century.

Climbing from the cable car, we ascended the few dozen crumbling steps leading to the summit of the hill and got our first full, unobstructed view of the castle. We followed more stone steps, which continued to the front of the castle and its courtyard. A sign – written in German, French, Spanish, and English – greeted us at the entrance to the courtyard. Reading parts aloud, we learned that the hill on which the castle was built was called *Jettenbuhl* and was 640 feet above the Nectar River. The castle, although in ruins, was still considered one of the more impressive historic landmarks in Germany. We entered into the large, open courtyard, which contained four large granite columns flanking the doors of the castle.

As we crossed the open area, a sign caught my eye. It read "Heidelberg Tun" with an arrow pointing down an old stone stairway.

"I remember reading something about this Tun."

"What is it?" Dee asked.

"It has something to do with a wine cellar, but I can't remember anything else. Want to see?"

"Sure."

We took the stairs, descending into the depths of the castle, feeling the air grow colder and danker the closer we dove into the bowels of the medieval structure. As we reached the last step, a sign guided us into a cellar holding the biggest wine vat in the world. It was enormous – probably twelve to fifteen feet high – with a capacity to hold 58,000 gallons of wine. It was constructed in 1751 from 130 oak trees. A small sign written only in German was attached to the side of vat, and even with the aid of my German-American dictionary, we finally decided that we couldn't translate the message.

We ascended into the bright daylight and meandered through the sunny courtyard with mingled architecture and statues from various eras. Exploring narrow, quiet passageways, we followed the crumbling stone wall to an area where we got our first breathtaking panorama of the city below. Orange-brown rooftops gave way to soaring church steeples, reverberating with the sounds of their bells.

Even though the front courtyard had had no flower gardens, the area behind the castle was a vast array of blossoming color. Adorned with statues and fountains, the gardens were spectacular, and, as always, the landscape filled with symmetrical designs of shrubs and flowers was Dee's favorite place.

"Just look at the gorgeous gardens. Isn't it amazing that the Europeans maintain these fantastic gardens at a ruined castle?" Dee was already focusing on giant white mums and an unusual blue blossoming shrub. With camera in hand, she was snapping close-up shots of every flower.

"You know, in America we would have this castle torn down and a modern building put in its place," Dee added, moving closer to a flowering rose bush, lavished with huge, scarlet velvety petals.

I nodded, knowing that Americans loved coming to Europe to view history and ancient monuments. Intrigued with the old – because we only saw modern sites in the

States – Americans were drawn to these ancient ruins, spending hours strolling through the gardens and soaking up the ambiance.

We left the ruins that afternoon only after I nearly knocked myself out. A small opening in the brick wall – large enough for the insertion of a cannon used to protect the castle – allowed enough room for my head, but misjudging its size, I raised up too soon. I can still feel the painful thud as I put head-to-brick, acquiring an egg-sized knot on my crown.

We spent the next day ambling through the cobble stone streets of that historic, relaxed, university city. Large market squares were edged with colorful outdoor cafes and the picturesque castle ruins overlooked everything. Heidelberg somehow avoided the bombs of WWII, and so the intricate Baroque architecture found on many of the old building facades was original. There were no twentieth-century reconstruction look-alikes – the old city was truly authentic.

In the midst of the "Old Town," we found a small outdoor café and enjoyed an afternoon coffee. Situated in the middle of a street leading to the university, the café was home to a crowd of German students, chatting and laughing behind steins of beer. All of them had textbooks in front of them, but no one was studying. As their laughter reverberated off the walls of the tiny café, it was carried up and down the street as passersby looked in, jealous of the students' youthful, carefree freedom.

We sat and observed the students for perhaps half an hour, enjoying the sound of their German language and the genuine laughter, which reached peaks and then subsided as steins were raised to their lips. As we left, a trio with accordions appeared, and as we meandered down the street, we could still hear the festivities flowing into the afternoon air as singing and clapping sounded in harmony with the German polka music.

* * * * * * * * * * *

Despite our love of Heidelberg, early the next morning a thick fog and cold drizzle drove us to the decision of leaving for France. While packing to leave Frau Hoffman's, we anticipated asking her for some boiled eggs to take along on the train. By now, Dee had also learned to enjoy a mid-morning snack of boiled eggs and European rye crackers, so we decided to request enough boiled eggs for several days.

Frau was accustomed to making us four eggs – two apiece – each morning for our breakfast, but now we had to break the news that we needed twelve eggs this morning.

We were getting accustomed to communicating with hand signals, plus my German vocabulary had increased from two words to at least ten words now.

One of the essential words I had learned was egg – *ei*. I hadn't located the words for raw egg, but then I was always on the lookout on the menu for anything that had an unusual inclusion with the word egg. *Kraftbruhe mit ei* was a very suspicious dish from which I would shy away. I had no clue of the contents of the dish, but I did know that *mit ei* meant "with egg." For all I knew, it could be a floating, raw egg.

In addition, raw hamburger – *tartar*—was a popular dish in Europe. Instantly, I filed that word at the top of the list of essential German vocabulary words, never to be forgotten. No *tartar* would ever pass through my lips. A raw egg could be tolerated if absolutely necessary, but I made sure that I didn't get any raw cow.

"Frau, we need *eier* this morning," I attempted to communicate.

Frau nodded sweetly and smiled in acknowledgement. She held up four fingers. Dee and I looked at each other and then proceeded to break the news.

"No, Frau, we need twelve *eier,*" I said.

Dee now decided to take part in this exhibition. She repeated the word "twelve" as Frau remained expressionless, obviously not comprehending.

Not knowing the German word for twelve, Dee started her pantomime. "Frau, five, ten, twelve."

I looked at Dee as she held up five fingers, five again, and then two as if demonstrating to one of her grade school children.

Frau suddenly caught on and burst into laughter. She held up ten fingers and then two more and continued to laugh until tears were running down her cheeks.

"This obviously is a first request for twelve eggs," I whispered, laughing at Frau Hoffman's reaction as she slapped her knees in response to our request.

After Frau started to gain control, she again held up ten fingers and then two. We nodded, and she burst again into a fit of laughter.

"Guess we've made her day, Dee. We'll probably be the topic of conversation when she chats with her German lady friends."

Suddenly a horrifying thought struck me, "You *do* think she'll boil them, don't you?"

"Oh, yeah, we never received raw eggs from Frau," Dee giggled.

Frau was still laughing as she turned to go into her kitchen to prepare our eggs.

We finished packing, paid for our room, and extra eggs – all warm and obviously cooked – and hugged Frau. "*Auf wiedersehen, Frau,*" we both said as we grabbed our luggage and waved, descending the four flights of stairs. My neon bag remained partially unzipped to accommodate the latest addition of twelve freshly cooked eggs.

"So we're headed for Paris?" Dee asked as we walked to the train station, dragging our suitcases in the cold drizzle that continued under a completely overcast sky.

"Yeah, if that's okay with you."

"Oh, yeah, that's fine," Dee replied. "At least you know some French and can communicate a little," she added.

"Yes, I can ask for eggs in French," I said with a broad smile. Even with that knowledge, our experiences with eggs were still not over.

Chapter 10

Roosting in the Rafters

We located the train schedule in the railroad station. With fifteen minutes to spare before the train left for Paris, there was time to enjoy a cup of coffee at the depot cafe.

"J.J., look at those Germans eating bratwurst and drinking dark, German beer for breakfast. Can you believe that?" Dee asked, a bit horrified at the thought.

"Well, Dee, anyone who eats raw eggs could just as easily eat bratwurst and drink beer for breakfast. It doesn't seem too bad," I said with a smug grin.

Dee threw me a disgruntled look as I added, "I'm just taking your advice and trying to adjust to the German customs. Seriously, though, I never was at my grandma's for breakfast. Now I wonder what she ate. Surely, it was normal food, don't you think?" I asked.

"Don't know," she shrugged. "I'm Italian, you know. I was never around the crazy Germans who eat brats and drink beer for breakfast. We eat pasta and drink wine at all meals," she winked.

Because European trains leave exactly on time, we watched the clock closely. With five minutes to spare, we gathered our luggage and headed toward our train track.

As we boarded, we noticed couchettes, berths designed for sleeping. With two beds to a couchette, they looked comfy and cozy. Adding to the appeal were fluffy pillows and billowy down-filled comforters, which topped each berth.

"You know, Dee, sleeping on the train one night would be a great way to save on hotel costs. Why not plan on that when we leave Paris?"

"Great idea. If we would leave Paris at 7 o'clock in the

evening, we could arrive at our destination in the morning – with a free night's sleep," Dee replied, cheerfully, also thinking of saving money.

Our plans were laid for our departure from Paris, and we thought we were quite clever – no money would be spent on a hotel or pension. Little did we know that it would prove to be one of the worst – and sleepless – ideas of the trip.

We didn't get to Paris that night. With no schedule to keep, we stopped in German villages along the way. They held old-world charm, and we stayed a week longer in Germany than intended.

In fact, we even took one train in the opposite direction from Paris so that we could visit Ulm, Germany, home of Albert Einstein. Fellow travelers had told us of this village, tucked into a valley, away from the hustle and bustle of life, and we decided it might be worth the detour.

Located on the Danube River, Ulm dated back to 854 and still contained remnants of ancient walls and towers. The city housed one of Europe's most magnificent early Gothic cathedrals, built in 1377. Capable of seating 30,000 people, the interior was massive and second largest ecclesiastical structure in Germany – with only Cologne Cathedral surpassing it.

With a spire of 161 meters, it was the highest steeple in the world. Climbing the 768 steps to the top, we were rewarded with a spectacular panoramic view of not only Ulm, but also a vista of Alpine ranges in all directions.

It was in Ulm that I lost a filling in a tooth and visited my first and only European dentist. He spoke no English so the hotel clerk acted as an interpreter via telephone. In those days, German dentists liked to crown any tooth that contained a cavity. Even a miniscule cavity was rewarded with a crown. Of course, I didn't know this, and it wasn't communicated to me in our three-way conversation. Before I knew it, a temporary crown topped my tooth. Later in the afternoon, the dentist called the hotel clerk giving directions for me to see a dentist immediately upon my return home. It was a costly tooth repair – requiring a permanent crown – when I returned to the States.

It was fifteen years later that I returned to Ulm to once again visit the enchanting village with the immense cathedral. My husband, children, and I would stay in a bed-and-breakfast provided by a sweet German couple, probably in their 70s. Stout, gray-haired, and ruddy cheeked, Alfred Schneider looked "very German." Frau – with her snow white hair pinned into a bun on top of her head – held a continual smile on her face and sparkles in her deep blue eyes.

The Schneiders didn't speak English, and my German vocabulary hadn't improved much, so again sign language and a German dictionary made our communication possible. We wanted scrambled eggs for breakfast, and even though we found the German word in the dictionary, the Schneiders didn't know how to make them.

Frau shook her head and lovingly took off her apron and put it on me, offering me her kitchen to prepare whatever we wanted. Hand-in-hand, they sat in the dining room, watching me whip up scrambled eggs and toast. Offering them each a plate, the Schneiders accepted and ate their first American breakfast with beaming smiles. As we left, we snapped their picture, which still remains in my photo album today, reminding me of the warmth that we felt from the special German couple in Ulm.

* * * * * * * * *

We sat on the train for seven hours, going from Ulm to Paris. It gave me time to reminisce about my initial love of France and especially Paris, which had become an icon to me even as a little girl. When I was about seven, a friend of my mom's had visited Paris and had brought me a little souvenir Eiffel Tower. It took a special place on my dresser so that each and every day I could look at it and dream. I was captivated by it. Why, I don't know.

And so when I entered high school, there was no doubt that I'd take French, and then I continued with the language for two more years at college. There was something about the French words – considered by some to be the ultimate romance language of Europe – that totally fascinated me. As I listened to nasal consonants that somehow sounded fantastically poetic and to flowing, aspirated vowels, which simply rolled off the teacher's tongue, I knew that I was "hooked." I had wanted to become submerged into the French culture, so enamored was I with the country and its language. I had longed to see Paris after my first week in French class and read everything that I could find on the culture and society of France. I had even gotten a French cookbook to try some high French cuisine. Unfortunately, my soufflés and crepes lacked some of the authentic French flair. Actually, they lack more than flair – possibly they lacked ingredients as well because they always turned out flat.

However, Paris – "The City of Light" – was the ultimate for me as I sat in French class. I could imagine the beautiful, enchanting, poetic language, flowing from the mouths of the Parisians, who sat in the evening drinking *café noir* at a fashionable outdoor cafe on the Champs Elysses. I was sure that a person could sit on that celebrated boulevard and watch all of the elite of Paris passing in their chic, black formal wear as they strolled to some high-society event. Surely, Paris must be an imaginary place in which time stood still and the world passed by somehow, leaving the city unscathed and unharmed from normal everyday life.

I looked at Dee who was entranced with the scenery, changing from hills topped with castles to green farmland and tiny, centuries-old French villages.

"Dee, can you remember the excitement of visiting Paris last year? It was our first European city," I reminisced, more to myself than to Dee. "I couldn't believe that we were seeing the Eiffel Tower – that we were really here. I had to pinch myself to make sure it wasn't all a dream."

Dee threw me a dubious look. "Well, I didn't see Paris quite as you did, J.J. Remember, I didn't speak French, and I felt totally confused the first few days. I really didn't like Paris."

"I guess I forgot that, Dee. For so long, it had been my dream to come to France. Undoubtedly, I was in my own little world."

"Nothing really mattered that first afternoon, J.J. because I went to bed, giving in to the jet lag rather than fighting it. Then when I did go with you to eat dinner that first night, I thought the French were rude and snobbish. Because I couldn't speak French, they seemed to look right *through* me instead of *at* me. Last year's trip to Paris was not that enjoyable for me. Hopefully, I'll see things differently this year."

"You loved the *sights*, though, didn't you? The Eiffel Tower, Notre Dame, Montmartre?"

"Yeah, but I wasn't in awe like you were. I should have bought a tour book before leaving the States and read about the history as you did," she smiled.

"I suppose that I was brainwashed before I even arrived in Paris," I continued. "I was in love with everything about the city, and *nothing* could have changed my feelings. If the French were rude, I wouldn't have noticed. People always said that the city was dirty. I didn't see it. Americans often thought that the French took advantage of us and would raise the price of the merchandise when we entered a shop. I didn't believe it. The love and fascination of Paris was cemented into my mind long before I ever set foot on European soil."

Dee was quiet, pondering a thought for a moment. "I

113

guess that last year, I felt, well, intimidated by the huge cultural difference. It was our first European city, and it was just all too much for me to comprehend or appreciate."

"Well, it's true that last year we both were intimidated at one time or another," I commented. "After all, we had never been out of the States except to Mexico and Canada. The European cultures were overwhelming."

I often tried to explain to people who hadn't traveled to Europe what the cultural experience was like. Allegorically, I related it to a large bird, scooping me up, swooping me across the ocean, and suddenly dropping me into an alien world, full of unknown, unfamiliar cultures. I was left there to fend for myself and discover the ways of old-world Europe with all of its quaint, yet charming sophistication. And it would all happen in a matter of hours – that is, if your plane didn't have any long delays on the runway while in the States.

* * * * * * * * *

As we rode the train across the countryside, we chatted, ate, and napped frequently, making up for any lost hours of sleep time. Arriving in Paris was a thrill. Quickly, we checked the hotel list when we arrived at the northern Paris train station – *Gare du Nord* – and again we found a hotel that was close.

Many European train stations seemed to attract a homeless population, who thrived on their pickpocket techniques. The Paris train depots were notorious for pickpockets as well as gypsies, so tightening security on our purses, we proceeded onto the busy Paris streets. Horns honked on all sides of us as the impatient French drivers attempted to maneuver through the jammed traffic on the Parisian streets. It seemed that cars buzzed from all directions, and we attached ourselves to the shirttails of a French couple crossing the street. "If we get hit, so do they" was my motto as we dodged the crazy city drivers.

The hotel was a small, well-kept hotel that was two blocks from the station.

"Dee, there's an elevator, too," I noticed as we waited to be helped by the *exquisite* male standing behind the desk.

"Elevators and eggs seem to top the list of conversation topics nowadays," Dee laughed, eyeing the hotel clerk for the first time.

"Yeah, and for good reason," I was quick to respond.

As the couple ahead of us left, the hotel clerk turned to us, and I decided to practice a bit of my French on the too-handsome-for-his-own-good Frenchman, named Jean-Paul.

"*Excusez moi, monsieur*," I smiled. "*Avez vous une chambre pour deux?*" I asked in my best French.

"Yes, I have a room for two," he grinned, responding in English. I had found in the past that if I attempted one sentence in French, then they would readily reply in English. It worked every time. However, if the proud French people could not squeeze a single word of their language from me, then my chances of communicating in English were null.

The price was right, the lobby was clean and neat, and Jean-Paul's beautiful French accent was enough to finalize our decision. We took the room without hesitation. Of course, the elevator was a definite plus, as the stairs looked steep and narrow. No tugging our suitcases up any god-awful lethal maze this time.

"Your room is 652, and the elevator is to your left, *mademoiselles*. Let me know if I can be of further service." Jean-Paul's award-winning smile spread over his face. We melted.

"*Merci, beaucoup, monsieur*," I replied.

I looked at Dee, whose eyes had a love-sick glaze as her fixated stare remained frozen on Jean-Paul.

"I've never seen such a gorgeous hunk," Dee whis-

115

pered, trying to pull her focus off Jean-Paul as we walked toward the elevator.

"He's married, Dee."

"What?"

"He's wearing a ring," I replied,

"You had time to look at his *hand*?" Dee questioned in shock.

"Well, one of us had to, and it couldn't have been you because you had the look of a love-struck puppy."

"Geeze, the best are always married or priests. It's just not fair," Dee mumbled.

"Is this hunk better than Hans?" I questioned, a gleam in my eye as I thought of her last fascination back in Holland.

"Hans who?" she grinned.

Dee reached the elevator first, and the look on her face changed. I knew there was a problem.

"J.J., it's a cubicle. There's room for one person as long as you don't have luggage!"

"You know, if only we could crawl into the heads of the European contractors and figure out what goes on with them when they construct hotels. The Dutch build hotel staircases with impossible S-curves just wide enough for stick-people with no luggage. The French make hotel elevators big enough for a petite lady and her clutch purse," I said, totally frustrated.

Dee still stood speechless, staring at the elevator, measuring three feet by three feet.

"Okay, Dee here's an idea," I continued. "I think that our luggage will fit onto the elevator. You get a head start up the stairs to the sixth floor. No, fifth floor because our room is 652, right?"

Dee nodded. "Yeah, what ever you say, J.J." She was probably still day dreaming about Jean-Paul.

"Anyway, I'll load the luggage onto the elevator and push the button so it'll stop on floor five. You unload the luggage. Meanwhile, I'll sprint up the stairs." I smiled, proud of my quick thinking.

"Okay, sounds like a plan. Give me a couple of minutes to get to the fifth floor," Dee replied, stealing a final glance at Jean-Paul, who flashed us another Hollywood, Crest-toothpaste smile.

I loaded the suitcases onto the elevator – the neon-green delicately balanced on top of the other three – pushed the button for floor five, and started my jaunt up the stairs. After the first flight, the lights went out.

"Timer-lights again," I chuckled, pushing the button for the lights as I reached the landing. I could hear stumbling above me along with giggles, leading me to believe that Dee too had encountered the dark stairs.

When I got to the fifth floor, my suitcases were sitting next to the elevator, and Dee was gone, obviously searching for Room 652. Retrieving my luggage, I called her name.

"Here, J.J., around the corner. You may want to prepare yourself, however."

"Oh, no, now what? Another clothes closet?" I questioned, panting from the jaunt.

"Well, not exactly. This time we're being housed in the rafters," Dee replied.

Peering into the room, my eyes focused on the ceiling, sloping at unbelievable steeple-steep angles on three of the four sides of the room.

"There's no way to stand up straight in this room unless you're a pigmy," I noted, wondering how any human could possibly build a room like this on purpose.

"Maybe there is another room available. We'll both have concussions if we get up in the middle of the night and forget that we can only crawl on all fours in our room," Dee added as she headed for the elevator. "I'll ask Jean-Paul," she smiled, getting into the elevator and pushing the "down" button.

"Hey, Dee, tell Jean-Paul that we're not birds, nesting. Besides, it must be pushing 150 degrees in there," I added, feeling the heat pouring out of the door.

I looked into the room again and had to chuckle. How could the Europeans get away with housing people in these attic cubicles and actually collecting a hotel fee for them? Walking to the window, I realized why it was so hot. There was another building a few feet away, allowing no air to circulate. Plus, the hot, Paris sun was directly overhead, sizzling the city into record-breaking temperatures.

Dee returned within five minutes. The expression on her face as she entered the room doused my hope of leaving this over-heated oven.

"This is the only available room tonight. Jean-Paul says that he may have a different room tomorrow night if the French couple in Room 204 leave. I asked about a fan, but they are all in use. That, too, he may have tomorrow night," Dee concluded in dismay. "Oh, by the way, you're right. He's wearing a ring." I smiled and nodded.

"Well, by tomorrow, it'll take more than a fan to revive us after a night in this torture chamber. We're going to have to leave the door open in order to get a little air circulation. But don't worry because we have a built-in burglar alarm if someone tries to rob us during the night."

"What do you mean?" Dee questioned.

"The ceiling – anyone taller than a three-foot dwarf would knock himself out if he came in unexpectedly," I replied.

Dee had started to giggle, already seeing the jovial side of this situation. I decided it was time that I lighten up and view every incredible, inconceivable situation as part of our European adventure.

Chapter 11

Not Another Egg Story

We dropped our bags into the room and retreated into the hallway, which was at least ten degrees cooler than our room. For the most part, European hotels had not yet been introduced to air-conditioning in the '70s, so we Americans had to toughen up to show we weren't "soft."

As I pushed the "down" button, I said half-heartedly, "Maybe there's hope after the sun goes down. The room may become bearable."

"Yeah, well, *maybe*," Dee replied dubiously as we squeezed into the elevator.

To Dee's regret, Jean-Paul was busy helping other guests as we left. "Let's find a place to eat," Dee commented as she coquettishly waved to Jean-Paul, who returned the gesture with a smile and a nod.

We were both hungry – eating seemed to be our favorite past time. We had munched while on the train, but it was now 5 o'clock. We decided to resort to a standby idea that we had used the previous year – going to a grocery store with a delicatessen. It was cheaper plus we could get exactly what we wanted – with no chance of getting raw eggs at the deli.

I had noticed a nearby, local grocery store, crunched between office buildings, which comprised most of the block. We strolled down the narrow street, which was never constructed for automobiles. Pedestrians and carts would have fit perfectly onto the tiny Parisian streets, laid out centuries before. The neighborhood grocery store had a wonderful selection of creamy cheeses, French bread, and fruit. A picnic dinner was our plan, and the area around the Eiffel Tower would be our place.

It proved to be a wonderful idea. It was a magnificent sight as we sat on the grass, looking up at the Eiffel Tower. The complex pattern of ironwork used to stabilize the Tower against high winds created a symmetrical design unsurpassed by other manmade structures. We sat, talked, and people-watched until the Eiffel Tower's lights flicked on at dusk, twinkling up and down the huge iron masterpiece, which – during its construction for the World's Fair in 1889 – was considered a monstrosity. Designed by Gustave Eiffel, it was meant to be only a temporary addition to the Paris skyline, and the Parisians were appalled by the horribly, ugly aesthetics of the structure.

"J.J., we didn't have time to go up in the Eiffel Tower last year. Let's go tonight."

"You know I hate heights, Dee. Why don't you go alone. I'll wait here."

"Look, the elevator is completely enclosed, and you don't have to look down. Come on. What do you say?" Dee urged. "It'll be an adventure."

"I don't know, Dee," I hesitated.

"Come on. Live a little," she urged.

"Well, okay," I replied, still skeptical. "First, though, let my food digest. I'd hate to upchuck in the elevator," I grinned.

As we sat soaking up the Parisian atmosphere, a young couple with two children sprawled onto the grass next to us. We watched as the French couple played with the little girl and boy – probably aged five and three – with such love and warmth. The children nestled and squirmed in the arms of their parents, showering their faces with kisses. Little hands reached out to touch and hold the big faces so gently. It was a true love affair between the children and their parents. They reminded me of lions playing with their cubs – so gentle was the affection and yet so tenuous and firm.

I wanted a family, but I knew I wasn't ready. Maturity

and self-confidence needed to precede a relationship like that – and yet the parents weren't much older than I was. *C'est la vie*, I thought. We all reach stages at different times in our lives. Right now I'm learning more about the world, foreign cultures, and life, I thought. Someday I'll have the opportunity to learn about the special person in my life with whom I'll share our children.

Dee poked me. "Hey, it's 9 o'clock. Let's get into line for the Eiffel Tower."

It was 9:30 when we finally got onto the elevator. There would be two stops before reaching the top, and at each, I begged to get off and see Paris from a less-frightening height than the 899-foot view from the third level. Dee was adamant about going all the way, and I wasn't getting off alone so I succumbed. Dee was right, however – the ride up was fine. It was smooth, and the aerial view of Paris coming alive in the early evening was magnificent.

As we arrived on top, I got my first glimpse of the whole of Paris aglow with millions of sparkling lights – it was spectacular. We walked all around, picking out some of our favorite places – the Louvre, Arc de Triomphe, Montmartre, Sacre Coeur, and the Etoile, all thrusting a glow into the dark Paris sky. The Seine River wound through Paris in serpentine style with dozens of cruise boats drifting through the ebony waters, giving tourists a glimpse of Paris at night when it was at its erotic best.

"I understand why Paris is called 'The City of Light,'" Dee commented after several minutes of being spellbound by the magnificent sight. "Look at the Etoile. The streets form a perfect star. Thus, the name Etoile, I guess, huh?" she grinned.

I had to admit that it was exciting, but after twenty minutes, it was all I wanted of heights, and I was ready to descend. However, there was one problem – during the twenty minutes that we were at the top, the elevator had broken down. The elevator operator said that because of technical difficulties, we would be delayed at the top.

"Isn't there another elevator?" I questioned in near panic.

"*Oui*, but it is broken, too, *mademoiselle*."

"I can't believe this. Probably, the elevators have been fine for fifty years, and tonight they chose to break down while I'm on top," I remarked to Dee in frustration as my eye caught sight of a staircase.

"Sir, may we use the stairs?" I asked, a ray of hope forming.

"No, sorry, *mademoiselle*. The stairs are being repaired. They can only be used in case of an emergency," he quickly replied.

"*An emergency!* Dee, don't you think this constitutes an emergency?" I knew that I may be over-reacting, but I couldn't help it. "If I have a seizure because of fear of heights, do you think they'll let me use the stairs?"

"Relax, J.J. It's going to be fine. Now, let's go back to the railing and look at the sights."

"No, Dee. No more sights for me. I'm standing right by the elevators, so I'm the first on when one has been repaired."

Dee shrugged as she sauntered back to the railing to get another glimpse of Paris.

Slowly, the minutes ticked by as I tried to remain composed. Wild thoughts bounced in and out of my mind – what if lightning struck us, an airplane collided with the Tower, or the steel just crumbled – kind of like blue cheese – because of too many people and too much weight at the top?

I looked over at Dee, who was perusing the Tower again. She snapped pictures with my camera as she gazed first on one side and then the other. She was obviously engrossed with the view, no longer concerned with my panic.

Forty-five minutes later, the elevator doors opened.

Admittedly, I was the only one cheering as I scrambled inside. Dee – still consumed with the scenery – looked up just in time to jump on as the doors closed. I would be a happy camper only when standing on solid ground again. As we descended, there were frantic images going through my mind of the elevator breaking down and getting stuck *between* the floors, never to move again. Within minutes, though, we were safely down – not, however, without perspiration beading on my brow and trickling down my cheeks.

"See, that wasn't bad, was it?" Dee asked as I caught up with her, heading for the ice cream stand.

"Yes, Dee, it was *awful*. And how can you think of eating?" I questioned as she stopped in front of the stand and pointed to the chocolate ice cream, holding up two fingers for a double scoop.

She shrugged, paid for the cone, and headed for a bench under the Eiffel Tower. I was still attempting to regain my composure, my insides knotted and shaking as Dee's tongue casually licked chocolate drips of ice cream as they dribbled down the cone. My eye caught sight of the elevator smoothly and effortlessly gliding up to the first level, and I wondered why I had been so intimidated – no horrified – by the ride. It looked harmless from ground level.

"Let's stroll to the Trocedero," Dee suggested as her tongue again shot out for a drip of ice cream, which she missed.

It was a ten-minute walk to the Trocedero, an elevated area that overlooked the entire plaza of the Eiffel Tower. It was the perfect spot for a picture – we could see the entire Eiffel Tower, aglow in the darkened Paris sky. I took a couple of pictures, one with Dee wearing a newly-acquired beret that she bought from a street vendor selling "authentic" Paris souvenirs. Frankly, I couldn't focus on eating or buying anything after the near-fatal experience – perhaps I was again exaggerating, I chided myself – atop the Eiffel Tower. I was truly attempting to enjoy the gorgeous picture-postcard view of the Tower as seen from the Trocedero, but in reality my stomach was still churning, and my knees felt weak.

"Let's go back to the hotel, Dee," I suggested.

She threw me a questioning glance but didn't argue.

We decided to take the metro, located two minutes from the Trocedero. Typical of the underground subway in the summertime, it was extremely hot and crowded.

"I wonder if our hotel room is any cooler than this metro, Dee. We're in big trouble if it isn't. I may just sleep in the hall," I said as the subway stopped, and a dozen more people pushed their way into the already-crammed car.

"However, I'd rather suffer with the heat than the height of the Eiffel Tower," I smiled.

It was midnight when we reached our room. Fortunately, it had cooled down a little from the stifling afternoon heat, but with no air circulation, it was still unbearable.

"I'm going to leave the door open, Dee. No one is going to find us in the attic rafters of this hotel. We're in a corner that probably the maid doesn't even know exists."

* * * * * * * * * *

It was a restless night as we baked in the oven. Rolling and tossing in the perspiration-soaked sheets, I awoke four or five times to get a glass of water in an attempt to cool down. As morning dawned, we looked up at an inviting, overcast sky.

"Hey, it's cloudy. That should help with the heat index," Dee commented, looking up at the small patch of gray sky, visible between the buildings that surrounded our hotel. Our hope was that the outside air was cooler than our room, still stifling with little circulation.

"Let's get a quick shower and have something to eat. Is the breakfast room on the ground floor?" Dee questioned.

"Yeah, I think so. I've been practicing my French so I can order eggs this morning. Remember last year I had a problem being understood? I guess, my French accent on the word eggs was not entirely perfect," I smiled.

"Are you sure that it's *just* on the word 'egg' that your pronunciation is off?" Dee teased. "I remember last year when we had trouble..."

"Okay, okay. I try, though, and that's the important thing," I retorted.

As we reached the breakfast room, neatly arranged tables greeted us. Rolls, coffee, tea, and juice were arranged on each table, which was artistically decorated with a lace tablecloth, linen napkins, and a vase of freshly cut flowers. A tiny, French lady dressed in black and white was bustling about the room, cleaning up a table that a couple had just left.

"Wish me luck in asking for eggs," I whispered.

"Yes, eggs have been a raw topic lately – pardon the pun," Dee smiled. Chuckling, I turned to the waitress.

"*Pardon, madame. Avez vous les oeuves?*"

"*Pardon, mademoiselle?*" she questioned with a puzzled look.

"*Les oeuves.* Eggs. *Les oeuves, madame,*" I repeated more slowly.

Dee was watching me with a smug smile as I struggled with the precise French pronunciation for eggs. I made the attempt several more times with the word "oeuves," trying to comprehend how I could mispronounce a small French word that seemed so innocent.

To my astonishment, suddenly, the lady's face lit up, and she excitedly said, "*Oui, oui.*"

"Wow! I finally pronounced *oeuves* correctly," I whispered to Dee.

However, instantly, all hope was crushed, as the little French lady grabbed me by the hand, pointing towards a picture on the wall. Too shocked to resist, I allowed myself to be pulled along by the excited waitress.

"*Ici, ici,*" she said excitedly.

I tried to glance at Dee over my shoulder, hoping she was tagging along, too; but, no, she was sitting comfortably in her seat – watching the newly evolved egg escapade.

"What is the picture?" I heard Dee ask in a whisper.

I stood for a moment, staring at it – totally confused. I didn't answer her, but I could already hear Dee laughing as she knew the inquiry for eggs had not been successful but wondered what I *had* asked. I, too, was wondering the same thing.

The lady continued to chatter in French, apparently thinking every word was understood as I tried to smile and nod with interest as she pointed out features in a painting of a wild animal.

"J.J., what is the picture?" Dee insisted again, trying hard to control her laughter so the lady – who was so politely showing me each distinct feature of the animal – wouldn't hear her.

I tried to whisper to Dee as the lady continued to deliver a full description – all in French, of course, "It's a picture of some kind of spotted animal – maybe a jaguar or leopard. I don't know – maybe it's a lynx. She must have thought I asked her about a wild animal." I threw Dee a feeble smile as I attempted to stay focused on the picture.

However, it was all I could do to remain straight-faced as the lady – trying to be so hospitable – finally stopped mid-sentence in the one-way conversation only because her helper called from the kitchen.

"*Oh, excusez moi, mademoiselle,*" she said apologetically, rushing toward the kitchen.

Going back to the table, I collapsed with laughter until I had tears running down my cheeks. Dee had to get up to see the picture for herself as she, too, wiped tears from her face.

"What exactly did I say!" I exclaimed. "What the heck is the correct French pronunciation for eggs? Obviously, I'm not getting any eggs – raw or cooked – for breakfast this morning."

Chapter 12

Leaping the Metro Wall

The rest of our morning was spent at Montmartre – the highest, most picturesque hill in Paris, which is a mecca for Parisian artists who sit day and night and create magnificent, original oil paintings, depicting not only the most memorable sights of Paris but also the places off-the-beaten path that are steeped in old-world magnetism – a café window with a bike leaning against its two-hundred-year-old building that has paint peeling away in large chunks; flower boxes trimmed in wrought iron and adorning a window of an old house that has plaster chipped from hundreds of years of abuse. Mobs of tourists ascend the hill each day to visit the charming, quaint area and buy the paintings that will keep Paris alive for them even when they return home.

Gathering in some of the open, spacious parts of the village square, the tourists find talented, quick-portrait artists, bargaining to draw a portrait. After dark, Montmartre comes alive with bordellos, cabarets, and other exotic places, all contributing to the ambiance of one of Paris' most popular tourist sites.

I thought about the previous year when Dee and I both had a portrait drawn. We waited in line for half an hour for a young artist, Jacques, who seemed to have talent. He had a knack for getting the eyes and mouth exact, which was important. He took 45 minutes to sketch both of our portraits in charcoal, sprayed them so they would be preserved, and wrapped them in cellophane. When we returned home, we had the portraits framed for our parents and surprised them at Christmas. My parents found a place in the front hall for the special Paris gift.

We sat for two hours and thoroughly enjoyed watching

the artists sketch or paint their masterpieces as tourists bargained for the best price. We sipped drinks at the chic outdoor cafes and shopped in the dozens of souvenir stores located on the hills and cobblestone streets of Montmartre, which still preserved the atmosphere of pre-war Paris. One of the shops contained nothing but posters, and I was enthralled by the racks of Parisian scenes depicted on the posters. I wanted some for my classroom and searched for half an hour for the perfect ones. The sales clerk – tall, dark, and handsome with no accent – helped me with my findings.

"Your English is perfect," I concluded as he found a tube in which to put the four posters I was buying. For a moment, I wondered how I would possibly squeeze another poster tube into my luggage. I decided to ponder that problem later.

"I'm Canadian – Alex," he smiled, extending his hand. "You're Americans?"

"Yes," I answered as Dee and I shook his hand. "How long have you been in Paris?" I questioned.

"For three years. My mother was French-Canadian, and on a whim I came to visit an uncle in Paris and stayed."

"So you must like it here?" Dee questioned.

"I guess I'm here to stay – married a French girl," Alex smiled.

"Well, I guess so," I grinned back to him. "Has she been to Canada with you to visit your parents?" I immediately wished I hadn't asked – the inquisitive side of me always made me seem nosey.

But Alex answered quickly. "Actually, we leave in a week for Quebec. I haven't been back in three years so I can't wait. They'll meet Daniella for the first time, and she's so nervous. I have four brothers and five sisters in Canada, and she wonders how she'll fit in. I tell her to relax," Alex concluded with a grin as he rang up the order. "Are you girls here on holiday?"

"Yes, and we love Paris, especially Montmartre," I answered as I picked up my tube and change.

"Have fun back in Canada," Dee said with a wave as we exited the store. A young girl was just entering the shop with coffee, and I caught a glimpse of Alex embracing her. Daniella, I thought, as I turned to catch up with Dee.

We followed the narrow, winding road around the hill until Sacre Coeur Basilica came into view. It was lovingly called "The White Dove of Paris" by the Parisians because of its brilliant, white-stoned structure. The beautiful church was built in the late 1800s after the Franco-Prussian War. Catholic businessmen promised to build a magnificent church if God would spare France in the war. Sacre Coeur was the fulfillment of that vow.

We sat on the steps of the Basilica overlooking the vast metropolis of Paris as the bell tower – with one of the biggest, heaviest bells in the world – echoed the start of morning mass.

"This view is so awesome. It's almost more spectacular than the view from the Eiffel Tower," Dee remarked. "I think that Montmartre is my favorite attraction in Paris. It's just the essence of the city."

"It's certainly safer up here than on top of the Eiffel Tower. There's no elevator on which to get stuck!" I grinned. "But you're right, Dee. Montmartre has everything that a tourist thinks of when trying to imagine Paris – painters, cafes, shops, mimes, and old, winding streets. Best of all is the spectacular view of the Eiffel Tower."

We sat on the steps, soaking up the ambiance of the bustling Paris morning and basking in the warm sun. With mass having started, we knew we couldn't enter the Basilica, but cemented in our minds from the previous year was the great mosaic of Christ dominating the chancel. I remembered the spiral staircase with the sustained, multi-colored glass gallery below it, which depicted Christ's life. I wished I could get one more glimpse of the rainbow of

131

colors found in that glass gallery, but it would not happen on this morning.

Eventually, we decided to make the steep descent down the one-hundred-fifty steps, leading from the top of Montmartre to the bottom of the hill. Half way down, I stopped to snap a photo of the picturesque ascension of flights of stone steps leading upward, with the Basilica at the top. Pocketing my camera, I said to Dee, "You know, I need to find a bathroom."

"Oh, there's a porta-potty down here at the base of Montmartre. I saw it on the way up. I need to use it, also." As we reached the bottom, Dee pointed to a small, circular structure with an automatic door. "There it is," she said.

We had seen porta-potties in various places in Paris, but we had never used one. Now, as we got closer, I noticed that it required a franc.

"I guess when my franc is deposited, the door will open," I remarked, searching for change in my purse.

Dropping the franc into the slot, the door revolved automatically.

"Cool. Hope it closes, too, when I get in there," I commented. Dee giggled as she stood watching. "Hold my poster tube, Dee. Don't let anyone snatch it, " I grinned as the door closed.

Once inside, I found a button to push to close the door, and a different one to open it again when I wanted out. The explanations on the buttons were written in both French and English, so someone like me couldn't make a mistake. Good thinking on the part of the French, I thought. At least they must have had "thinking" contractors constructing the porta-potties even though the less-than-desirable ones worked on the European hotels, stairways, and elevators.

Emerging, I suggested to Dee, "Hey, do you want to go in while the door is still open? You can save your franc."

Dee hesitated, "No, I better not. You never know with these Frenchmen – maybe the door won't open again, and

I'd be stuck in there,"

"Good point," I said as I let the door close automatically. As it clicked shut, we immediately heard the sound of a shower – from *inside* the porta-potty!

"Oh, my gosh. Now I remember reading that the porta-potties self-sanitize after people have used them. They are completely washed down with anti-bacterial soap and water. You would have had a free shower, Dee, if you had decided to go in without paying. That would have been a priceless experience – and a priceless photo when you emerged, soaking wet!"

"Gosh, just imagine me in there right now – sanitized from head to toe," Dee said with a tinge of horror in her voice.

"That really would have been worse than getting raw eggs!" I chuckled.

* * * * * * * * * *

The next few days were spent meandering through the streets of Paris, in and out of boutiques, artisans' shops, cafes, and alleyways. Eventually, we entered into the *Marais* district, which instantly became another of our favorite areas of Paris. Originally, a place of royal residency, it was abandoned during the French Revolution and descended into an architectural and cultural wasteland. Resurrection of the *Marais* began in the 1960s with buildings attaining new life as art galleries, chic boutiques, cultural centers, and airy outdoor cafes. Grand mansions were renewed into hotels and museums, and *Place des Vosages* resumed its importance as a magnificent park, lined on all sides with 400-year-old houses, which had deep slate roofs, dormer windows, and beautiful arcades.

We met Tim Billington, an Englishman, at *La Chop*, a quaint, timbered restaurant that opened onto a lush, green courtyard, and we immediately joined him in conversation.

Tim was thirtyish, tall – over six foot – and a lawyer in London. He and his wife were "on holiday" in France. His wife had taken ill that evening, so he was dining alone and asked us to join him at his table. He was a person who we felt we had known in some other time or space, and conversation flowed easily.

Tim – like Hans and Sarah whom we had met in our previous weeks abroad – seemed to have a clear focus on life and knew where he was going. Growing up in the poorer section of London, he matured early. He went to work at fourteen in a grocery store for money to support his habit of reading. By age 24, he had made his way to Oxford University, graduating top in his class. His wife, now pregnant with their first child, managed their budget well enough so that they could afford a down payment on a small bungalow in the outskirts of London. I envied Tim for his accomplishments.

We mulled over various topics as we savored our seafood delicacies, the specialty of the day. Somehow, though, our conversation turned to WWII. I probably instigated the topic because of my interest in the Holocaust. One question had always plagued me, and Tim seemed the right person to ask for clarification.

It seemed to me that there had been a shift of European attitudes toward the Americans since WWII. During the war, there were throngs of underfed, war-torn Europeans, waving deliriously to the GIs as they came into town in their jeeps. Readily and eagerly, the European nation accepted our help. Now, however, the current feelings toward their past heroes was often overt dislike. Of course, I realized that many events had occurred since the war to recolor situations – Vietnam and the Cold War. However, we *did* come to save Europe during WWII. Why did so many Europeans snub – or maybe hate – Americans today?

Tim thought about the question for only a second and looked me straight in the eye with the answer. "Yes, you did save us, but we *young* people still ask – because our *parents* have always asked – *what took you so long?*"

I felt stunned – was that the answer? I pondered it quickly. He was right, of course, because it was all a delayed reaction on the Americans' part. We had waited years before we entered the war and only then because of the Japanese attack on Pearl Harbor. We had let the Germans totally eradicate so much of Europe and murderously annihilate millions of Jews, and we sat in the comfort of our homes, hearing of the decimation of a continent thousands of miles from us. We had hidden our heads in the sand like an ostrich, hoping that everything would go away. This entire past dilemma of the American attitude and WWII sat with the Europeans like a growing tumor – no explanation made it go away. For the first time, I had an answer to the question that had gnawed at me since my first visit to Europe – why Americans weren't favorites with many Europeans.

Leaving Tim that night, I felt a fraction of an inch closer to understanding what had gone on thirty years earlier on that soil, and also I had a clearer insight into European thinking. We departed like old friends, giving Tim a hug and wishing his wife and him well on their upcoming family. Exchanging addresses, we hoped to meet again someday in London. Years later, I called on Tim, his wife, Laura, and his young son, Samuel, when I visited London for a week. Our conversation that day in London was as if it had never ended from the night that Dee and I met him in the *Marais.*

A few more days were spent in side trips to French villages. We'd take the early train out of Paris and the late train back. Staying in the Paris hotel – by now we had been moved from the rafters to Room 204 – and leaving our luggage meant that we didn't have to manhandle the suitcases. We had only our purses and a daypack to carry. Plus, we had the opportunity to see all of the beautiful French coun-

135

tryside, fanning in all directions from Paris.

One of our favorite trips was to Chartres to see the Cathedrale de Notre Dame de Chartres. Representing one of the highest aspirations of the Middle Ages, the cathedral was noted for its architecture and sculptures, but most important were its stained glass windows. The cathedral's windows gave the world a new color – cobalt or Chartres Blue.

Standing in awe outside the main portal, we viewed some of the first flying buttresses to be constructed on a cathedral. Chartres Cathedral – being one of the world's greatest Gothic churches – ranks third in size in the world, succumbing only to St. Peter's in Rome and Canterbury Cathedral. Once inside, sculptures in long, flowing robes – all standing with Christ – depicts the Lord's second coming. And then there is the celebrated choir screen with its forty niches, each containing statues illustrating different aspects of Christ's life. Despite all the beauty of the statues, everything fades to the Chartres Blue windows. Transfixed by the light of the stained glass, which covers 3,000 square yards, the glass is unequaled anywhere in the world because of its mystical color.

Exploring the old town of Chartres (*Vieux Quartiers*) with the medieval cobblestone streets was a must after visiting the church. At the foot of the Cathedral, the tiny lanes contained gabled, medieval houses and ancient humped bridges, throwing the tourists into the French Middle Ages. We decided to sit at an outdoor café and order dinner before catching the commuter train into Paris.

One thing that I had started to learn when dining in Europe was the meaning of patience. We had three hours before catching our train, and most of that would probably be taken up at the restaurant – unhurried dining was the norm in Europe. The Europeans had a way of not rushing – of stopping to soak up the ambiance of the day or night. In America, of course, we were used to eating and running – so much to do in our busy, hectic schedules that a leisurely meal was not part of our daily lifestyle. We zipped from place to place – always trying to seize the next minute while the important moment at hand slipped away.

As I sat sipping on a drink, my mind wandered back to a time in childhood when I grasped each moment – took each memory and held it preciously. I didn't rush ahead, looking for the new and unusual but rather stopped and savored what was happening right then. Back then, the corner grocery store owned by Mr. Brookings held countless hours of entertainment for me. I went every day to sit on the floor and thumb through the comics. I read Dagwood, Beetle Bailey, and Mickey Mouse, and then I would decide on a special one that I could afford by Friday when I got my quarter allowance.

I would stand and gaze at the huge gumball machine stashed away in the corner of the store – giant red, yellow, blue, orange, and white jawbreakers, waiting for my penny so I could stick the huge succulent ball of sugar-coated gum into my mouth and let it plump-out my cheek, giving me a mump-like image.

Then, I'd stroll by the bins of fresh cookies, watching a mother put two soft coconut macaroons into a bag for her child. Caramel cookies were my favorite, and my mother always succumbed to buying one for me when she was along.

I could stand in Mr. Brookings' store for an eternity, it seemed, patience abounding – no reason to rush or hurry. This type of relaxed lifestyle now seemed to escape me as I restlessly sat in the Paris café, anxiously awaiting my food, wanting to hurry onto the next segment of the evening.

We couldn't hurry, though, because there is no rushing the French when it comes to dining. Languidly, we ate our meal of delicious onion soup covered with rich cheese, succulent chicken in a wine sauce, French green beans, and a wonderful chocolate mousse for dessert. We declined after-

dinner coffee as it was nearly time to catch the last commuter train into Paris.

* * * ** * * * * * *

For our last evening in Paris, we treated ourselves to sitting at a café in the exclusive Etoile district. For an hour, we
sat at a table on the Champs-Elysses, the widest, most famous boulevard in Paris, sipping soda and people-watching.
It was always an expensive glass of soda or wine because
this was Paris' most popular boulevard. Years later, I'd take
students to McDonalds on the Champs-Elysses in order to
affordably sit, drink a soda, and watch people But in the
'70s, no McDonalds existed in all of Paris.

"There's just nothing like sitting here and watching the
thousands of Parisians taking their nightly stroll. What
could be more entertaining," I remarked in the form of a
rhetorical question.

The gorgeous, old chestnut trees and the pavement col-
orfully bordered by multitudes of flowers added to the
beauty of the lighted theatres, cafes, and shops to which
hundreds of people thronged each day.

"Well, we've had a few 'entertaining' experiences so far
on this trip," Dee giggled, tongue-in-check, "but, you're
right. This is great fun."

She sat pondering for a moment. "I think that we may
get through this day without any adventure. After all, it's
almost time to return to the hotel, so what could happen
now?" Dee questioned, looking at her watch and yawning.
"I think that we're 'home free.'"

"Well, possibly," I agreed.

Our watches showed it was 11 o'clock, and since we
were at the far end of Champs Elysses, we decided to catch
the nearby metro and head for our hotel, which was located
at the other end of the boulevard. The Metro was, of course,
crowded, and we stood for the fifteen-minute ride to the

Charles de Gaulle stop.

As we exited the train, we climbed the stairs toward the upper level of the metro station, chatting about our latest findings at the Louvre, which we had visited earlier that day. While listening to Dee as we walked, I was also trying to figure out a puzzling situation. We were at street level, but why hadn't we found our exit?

"I loved that Monet we saw this afternoon. The colors were absolutely..."

"Excuse me, Dee. Hate to interrupt, but where's our exit? It seems we're going in circles. We passed this same advertisement five minutes ago," I remarked, pointing to a cinema ad.

"Oh, did we get off at the wrong metro stop?"

"No, this is Charles de Gaulle. It's the right stop, so what's wrong?" I questioned more to myself than to Dee.

Looking up, I caught a glimpse of a familiar sight. "Hey, look. There's the exit we want over there," I said, pointing in the direction of the sign *Sorti – Rue de Wagram*.

"You mean the one on the other side of that wall?" Dee questioned.

"Yes, that's exactly what I mean," I answered with a frown. "We should be able to get to it, though," I concluded, trying to fathom a solution to our problem.

We walked for another five minutes, returning to exactly the same spot and longingly looking over the wall at the exit we wanted.

"You know what must have happened?" I finally decided. "We got off on the wrong side of the train. There are doors on both sides of the train, and we could have exited from either, and we, of course, chose the wrong side. It's impossible for us to reach that exit – unless we could get back onto the train and get off on the other side," I concluded.

"But the train is gone," Dee noted.

"Yeah, exactly."

"So what do we do now?" Dee asked. One pregnant moment later, she added, "Jump the wall?"

I smiled at her factious suggestion, but nevertheless, after surveying the height of the wall, I decided it *was* a possible solution – and, as I saw it, the *only* solution.

"Well, maybe. It's about five feet high. What do you think?" I asked, trying to imagine if we could successfully accomplish the task.

"You have long legs, J.J. If you could get to the top of the wall, you could help pull me over," Dee grinned. Without further hesitation, she added, "Let's do it. Otherwise, we'll be walking in circles all night."

I walked to the wall, looking carefully at the height. Mentally, I tried to imagine lifting myself up. Could I accomplish that task? I hesitated a moment longer.

"Well, okay. Hold my purse and camera," I said, mustering courage. "Here goes."

After two feeble attempts, I successfully swung my leg up and then pulled myself so that I was sitting on top, straddling the wall. Giggling hysterically – I had decided by now that laughter was the best medicine during our ridiculous adventures – I looked down at Dee.

"Okay, hand me the purses and camera; then give me your hand."

It was difficult to get Dee to stand up straight in order to pull her up because she was laughing so hard.

I tried twice to pull her up without tumbling back down myself. Finally, a poor homeless person walking by took pity on us and gave Dee a push, placing her on top of the wall next to me.

A small crowd of locals had by now gathered to watch. Obviously, it was not an everyday occurrence, and I think back about what the French must have thought of us crazy Americans trying to leap the metro wall.

As we emerged unscathed on the other side, I grabbed my camera.

"Hey, wait a minute, Dee. I *have* to get a picture of this infamous wall that we just conquered. One more adventure photo to add to our album," I said, quickly snapping a picture that would take priority in my scrapbook of memories that was simply entitled "The Wall." Not the Berlin Wall but certainly a wall of consequences for us that night in the Paris metro station.

Chapter 13

Without *Une Reservation*

The next morning was spent at the Opera Quarter, which bustled with shoppers, theatergoers, stockbrokers, bankers, and tourists. Nineteenth-century grandeur still survived in the boulevards, buildings, and shops. The delightful, narrow shopping arcades – *les passages* – remained as a remnant of another era.

"There's the Opera House, Dee," I noted, pointing to the grand building resembling a giant wedding cake. "The ghost from *Phantom of the Opera* was supposed to have lived there," I added, overwhelmed before even seeing the inside.

"I know. This is so exciting, J.J.," Dee added, shading her eyes against the 10 o'clock sun, now peeking over the buildings.

As we entered the Opera, we were awestruck with the Grand Staircase, constructed of brilliant, white marble. "Wow," Dee whispered, wide-eyed and open-mouthed.

We slowly wound our way up the staircase to the first level, hardly able to take our eyes off the incredible domed ceiling, which was covered with mosaics. Every aspect was magnificent. As we reached the second level, I glanced at the pamphlet we were given at the door.

"This is called the Grand Foyer," I commented, trying to comprehend the elegance of the spacious area in which the opera goers would congregate at intermission.

We continued to the auditorium, which was a riot of red velvet, golden leaves, and cherubs. The magnificent chandelier, dripping with thousands of clear crystals, hung from the ceiling, and I thought of it unexpectedly crashing onto stage at the end of act one of *Phantom of the Opera*. We sat for probably half an hour in the velvet seats, listening to a recorded opera softly filling the room. It was difficult to pull ourselves from that unbelievable room. For over an hour, we surveyed the multitude of columns, friezes, and sculptures, housed in that magnificent structure, which has always been one of Paris' most stately buildings. In contrast to all of this elegance, I thought of the dark, mysterious passages beneath the Opera along with the misty, candle-lit underground lake. All were known only by the phantom and used when he escaped with Christine from the world above.

Outside, we sat on the steps, soaking up the sun and discussing our plans for the rest of the day. We had decided to take the night train to Spain that evening to save money on a night's lodging. Very clever on our part, we thought – no hotel costs, plus we would be in Spain upon awakening the following morning.

"I think we need to check out of the hotel by 12:30, Dee," I commented, remembering a sign that I had tried to decipher with my limited French.

"Well, okay. We can probably store our luggage at the train station until tonight," Dee suggested. "We did that one time last year."

"Great idea."

So by noon, we returned to our Paris hotel to check out. Unfortunately, Jean-Paul wasn't there. We had hoped to have one last glimpse of the Parisian hunk.

"He's probably at home having lunch with his wife and kids." I flashed Dee a smile as she grimaced at the thought.

After storing our luggage at *Gare du Nord*, we caught a commuter train to visit Versailles, the colossal palace with its vast gardens designed by Louis XIV. At one time the palace luxuriously housed 20,000 people while the rest of France was in the thralls of depression and starvation.

We entered the palace courtyard through Mansart's original gateway grille, which is surmounted by royal arms and opens unto the enormous Ministers' Courtyard. As we

144

walked closer to the palace, we encountered the Marble Courtyard, enhanced with pure marble paving, urns, busts, and topped with gilded balconies extending from the palace. Then entering through the palace's golden doors, we strolled through the magnificent rooms, decorated with splendid casings, unbelievable ceiling paintings, gilded trim on walls and furniture, and elaborate stone and wooden carvings.

The Hall of Mirrors was our favorite room with its crystal chandeliers, gild-trimmed walls, and seventeen beautiful, reflective mirrors, stretching 233 feet, the length of the room. Each mirror faced a tall-arched window, adding to the climax and splendor of the interior. All great state occasions had been held in this multi-mirrored room along with the ratification of the Treaty of Versailles in 1919, ending WWI.

"What a room," I said as we sat on a stone bench constructed under one of the windows overlooking the gardens. "And these formal gardens, fountains, and geometrically-shaped shrubs are incredible, Dee. I have to admit that the French know how to manicure their flowerbeds to perfection," I noted.

Looking down, Dee spied a stack of pamphlets. "Hey, here are brochures in different languages, describing the gardens. Here's an English one," she said, grabbing a two-page, colored pamphlet.

I continued to focus on the flowing fountains as Dee read, "'The Gardens of Versailles were laid out by the landscape artist, Andre le Notre. At the peak of their glory, 1,400 fountains spewed forth. Le Notre created the Garden of Eden down the middle of his landscape masterpiece using ornamental lakes and canals, geometrically designed flowerbeds, and avenues bordered by statuary. On the mile-long Grand Canal, Louis XV – imagining he was in Venice – used to take gondola rides.' Wow! What a place, huh?" Dee concluded.

"Magnificent, elegant, lavish – none of those words do this palace justice," I answered, now forgetting the incredible Hall of Mirrors and completely in awe with the splendor of the Gardens of Versailles.

We spent an hour meandering outside, viewing the luxurious life of Louis XIV and his queen Marie-Therese. Unfortunately, it was a fact that the two lived in an extravagant world, oblivious to the poverty of their country. When the frivolous queen was told that the peasants had no bread to eat, she replied with the statement, "Then let them eat cake." The palace and the royal lifestyle of Louis XIV and Marie-Therese understandably nearly bankrupted the rest of France, which was already in the height of a deep, dark depression.

* * * * * * * * * *

We returned to Paris in time to grab a sandwich, retrieve our luggage, and find a couchette on the Spanish-bound train, which would serve as our hotel for the night. It was 7 o'clock, and we were excited at the onset of a new adventure.

"Dee, look at these fluffy comforters and huge, plump pillows. What luxury! We should do this each time we move to a different city. This is going to be great."

We pulled our luggage in, finding room for it below and above our berths. It took both of us to heave my green bag over my bed. I left the heavier, brown suitcase below. Dee's luggage was starting to bulge with more souvenirs. Two sisters and a brother had acquired T-shirts in Paris, and another sister got perfume displayed in a glass Eiffel Tower. I wondered if anything made of glass was a good idea, but Dee seemed confident that it could survive the rugged train trips and flight back to America. If it didn't, her clothes would be drenched in enough Paris perfume to last a lifetime.

146

We settled into our "bedroom," instantly becoming accustomed to our lush surroundings. I glanced at Dee as she arranged two fluffy pillows, and I nestled myself under my comforter, tour book in hand. Browsing through the section on Madrid, I began to concentrate on the upcoming sights as the train departed from the Paris depot. I knew that Dee was excited about Spain – more excited than I. For some unknown reason, I had little desire to see Spain.

"Hey, Dee, what is it you want to see in Madrid?"

I could see only the top of her head and partially-opened brown eyes as she replied in a muffled voice, "The only things I really want to see are a bullfight and a flamenco dance. You know, I think…"

A light tapping at our couchette door interrupted Dee's thoughts. I crawled out of my cozy bed, carefully opening the sliding door far enough to peek out. I spied the train conductor, dressed in a navy blue uniform and hat, holding a stack of tickets. He started speaking French at a speed which I wasn't accustomed to understanding. Out of his fifteen-second speech, one essential word was understood: *reservation!*

"Oh, no, Dee," I whispered under my breath.

"What's the matter? What did he say?"

"I understood one word that is critical. I think we need a reservation to stay in this couchette."

Using my best French – and striving for the nasal sound – I asked, "Re-ser-va-se-on?"

"*Oui, mademoiselle. Avez-vous une reservation?*"

"*Non, monsiuer,*" I replied, letting my lip drop into a sultry pout in an attempt to win a little empathy. It didn't work. He continued on in rapid-fire French – it was not a sympathetic tone.

I nodded, saying "*Oui, monsiuer. Nous allons.*"

Dee was tugging at my sleeve. "What's going on? Do we have to leave?" she questioned.

"Yeah, we do. We have to pack our suitcases, kiss this

room goodbye, and look for a place that isn't reserved," I replied as the conductor left. I peeked outside the door, and for the first time, I saw the word "reservation" on the window of the compartment.

"I don't know how I missed this sign. Reservation is even spelled the same way in French as in English." Again I was chiding myself for my shortcoming.

With dispirited hearts, we packed our suitcases, and taking one last look at the posh couchette, we dragged our bags into the narrow hallway. We decided to leave them outside our door until we could find a "home" for the night.

There were four train cars going to Madrid. The car we were in had couchettes, and the other three cars had compartments with padded benches but no beds. Unfortunately, every window had a reservation sign on it.

"What do we do if we can't find a place to sleep?" Dee asked – as if I had been in this situation before and had an answer to that question.

"No idea. If no one has any more sympathy than the conductor that just threw us out of *our* room, then we'll end up sleeping in the aisle. A prayer might come in handy at this point."

"Who thought up this idiotic idea anyway?" Dee questioned.

"Me, of course. I guess I should have known it was all too good to be true – a free night's sleep in a comfy, cozy couchette. Sorry, Dee."

As we neared the last compartment in the fourth car, we noticed that there was no reservation sign.

"At last – a place to stay," Dee remarked with excitement.

I peered in. "Dee, don't get too excited yet. Have a look at this compartment. It looks as if the French ran out of wood and padding. There's only one bench, and it has no seat padding. The second bench is completely missing. No wonder it isn't reserved!"

"We have no choice, though," Dee said, looking with frustration at the dejected compartment – dejected and rejected for good reason.

We went back for our suitcases and lugged them through the four cars until we reached the woe-begone room that understandably was still unoccupied. Throwing our bags in, we closed the door behind us. Cold, empty, and stark – adequate words to describe our inadequate bedroom. Bewildered, we sat on the one bench – our luggage haphazardly tossed into the space that was supposed to contain another bench – trying to imagine sleeping arrangements for the night.

"Boy, we've got a problem – one naked bench without even a stitch of padding on it, and two of us to share it," I stated, humbled by the turn of events. "Having reservations for a sleeping berth seems like an incredibly unreasonable idea to me," I continued more to myself than to Dee as I persisted in reprimanding myself for my negligence of not checking into the situation before getting onto the train.

"Let's take turns on the bench," Dee suggested in more of an upbeat tone than I could have mustered. "You sleep on it until midnight, and I'll sleep on the floor. Then we'll trade." She gave me a warm smile, which made me feel even more guilty.

"Well, let me take the floor first, Dee. I got us into this mess."

"No, I want to get the worst over first," she grinned.

We searched for our jackets. Since it was getting dark outside, the air had a new crisp chill, partially because we were gaining altitude as the train ascended into the mountains. Within the next few hours, three "f" words would adequately describe our room's temperature – frigid, frosty, and freezing.

We tried to get settled with me on the twelve-inch-wide wooden bench, and Dee on the hard, cold floor, covered with her jacket and huddled against our suitcases, as if they offered some sort of sanctuary. At 11:30, I woke up, shivering because of a brisk draft coming through the window.

"Dee, are you awake?" I touched her to make sure she was warm – no frozen corpse yet.

She turned over and groaned.

"I think my nose has frostbite. Are you okay?" I questioned.

"Is it still summer or have we passed over the equator into winter?" Dee asked as she sat up rubbing her hands together. "Maybe we missed Madrid, and we're heading for the South Pole." She still possessed her sense of humor so that was a good sign, I thought. "Why is it so darned cold?"

"I don't know, but when the French ran out of wood and seat padding for this compartment, they also ran out of window sealant. The cold air is literally whizzing through that window," I said, pulling my jacket closer around me. "Let's try to find another compartment. Maybe someone has gotten off the train by now, and we can nab his reserved spot."

"Fat chance of that happening," Dee replied, searching her pockets.

"What are you looking for?" I asked.

"I'm searching for mittens," she snickered. "My hands are freezing," she replied, digging her hands further into her pockets for warmth.

Leaving our luggage, we went in search of a new home for the remainder of the night. Curtains were pulled on all the compartments – a sure sign that they were occupied.

"J.J., I think there's a room here at the end of this car with the curtains open," Dee called, jaunting ahead of me. "Never mind," she said as she got to the room. "It has a reserved sign on it." There was definite dismay in her voice.

"Yes, but there are no passengers or luggage in there," I said, peering in. "Let's take a chance. All that can happen is that we get thrown out and have to return to our compartment bound for Siberia."

Returning for our luggage, we dragged them down the hallway, sneaking into the vacant compartment and quickly pulling the curtains.

"Well, there are no beds, but there are two fully padded benches. At least, we don't feel like complete outcasts," I remarked. "And it's much warmer in here."

"Hopefully, my hands will thaw out by morning," Dee added with a smile. "Anyway, let's try to get some sleep. We both have *something* that resembles a bed."

We curled up on the two benches, luggage stuffed below. With our jackets snuggled around us, we slept.

Sometime during the night, I felt someone at my feet and realized that we had two visitors sitting at the ends of our benches. Frankly, we were so tired that – in the middle of the night – we didn't care who they were as long as we weren't told to move. They never told us if they had paid for the room or had just sneaked in as we did, and not understanding the language, we never asked. At any rate, we slept until the warm, Spanish sun started to shine through the train window.

We learned several lessons on the train that night. One was that going south doesn't necessarily mean getting warmer – especially in the Spanish mountains on a night train. And most importantly, we learned that *une reservation* is an essential detail if you are going by Eurail. As we were leaving the train in the Madrid depot, I snapped a picture of the still-deserted one-bench compartment. In later years, it provided us with many laughs, and that section of my photo album was simply entitled "Night Train to Madrid."

Chapter 14

The Educational, Cultural Bullfight

Exiting from the train in Madrid at 9 o'clock, we were met with the hot morning sun as the high temperature and humidity curled Dee's hair into tight ringlets. It was difficult to imagine how it could have been so frigid on the train during the night.

"Madrid had better be special, Dee," I commented as the heat and humidity hit us in the face. "It must be over 100 degrees. Refresh my memory as to why we came here."

"For the bullfight and flamenco dancing."

"Oh, right. Hate to break the news to you, but I can't handle a bullfight. You know I'm an animal lover."

"I knew you would be too much of a wimp to go to the bullfight. You're too soft-hearted. I think that the bullfight will be an educational and cultural experience. It's okay, though; I'll go alone," Dee said in a flippant manner. "But you'll go to a flamenco dance, won't you?"

"Oh, sure. No problem," I replied, tugging my suitcase and chartreuse carry-on, which again got long, unusual stares as I exited the train.

I felt confused with Dee's decision of going to the bullfight. She was also adverse to animal cruelty, but she possessed that stoic determination to experience the unfamiliar and what she considered – at this moment, at least – an educational adventure of Spain.

As we entered the main terminal of the train depot, I remarked, "Dee, look at these men and women with signs advertising, 'rooms for rent.' I read somewhere that many Europeans rent spare bedrooms to tourists. Do you think renting a room from one of them might be a worthwhile idea?"

"Maybe. That's a nice looking older gentleman standing over there. Look at his sign. 'Room for rent. Short distants from station. 400 peseta a pearson. Brekfast. Have wife.'"

We both laughed, realizing "wife" was undoubtedly added to help innocent, unsuspecting young females like us feel safe.

"The sign *written* in English is a sure indication that he doesn't *speak* English – only Spanish. Someone else probably wrote the sign for him – misspelled words and all," Dee chuckled.

"He looks nice – elderly and safe – and the room is cheap enough." Quickly I figured the price in my head. "I guess that 400 peseta is about $3.50 or $4.00. Let's look at it. We can always change our minds," I suggested, walking toward him, dragging my suitcase, carry-on slung over my shoulder. How I ever escaped having a torn rotor cuff, I'll never know. Youth was on my side, I guess.

As we approached him, the gentleman tipped his hat, revealing a thick head of pure white hair. We smiled, nodding our heads "yes." His full-faced smile was endearing as he motioned to us that he would help with our luggage, but we declined. After making it up the staircase-to-hell in Holland, we could walk a short distance on flat ground in Spain. Besides, I didn't want to be responsible for an elderly man getting a hernia from my luggage.

The gentleman, Senor Castillo, and his wife had a modest flat on the second floor with an extra bedroom. Senora was a tiny, petite woman, wearing a blue housedress, trimmed with Spanish lace around the sleeves. The two were so cute together – obviously, still in love after many years of marriage. Senor stood with his arm around his wife as we surveyed the room.

It was small with twin beds placed near the window for maximum air circulation. Colorful, red and white flowered curtains were tied back, revealing a street of apartment buildings similar to the Costillo's. A small table, lamp, and, of course, a large vase of tiny blue flowers completed the décor.

"Looks great, Dee. What do you think?"

"I say that we should go for it."

We were right – neither of the Castillos spoke English. No problem, though, because we had survived our experience with Frau Hoffman in Germany, we could manage with the Castillos.

We nodded and handed him 800 peseta apiece – two nights' stay – and went into the room to unpack. Senora Castillo motioned us to follow her as she showed us the shower, realizing we had just gotten off the train and probably wanted to bathe. She was right about that.

She set the thick, red and white striped towels and washcloths in the bathroom, flashing a smile as she left us alone. After showering and freshening up, we felt revived and decided to go in search of breakfast.

The day was spent exploring Old Madrid, starting with the shops in *Puerta del Sol.* This was one of the city's most popular spots, with crowds of people converging on the square. Originally, this site had been occupied by a gate-house and castle and later a succession of churches. Now, it was just the center of the café society and fashionable shoppers. This was the heart of Old Madrid and was absolutely steeped with historical sights and legacies.

An austere, red brick building occupying one side of the square was the city's original post office, built in 1760. During the 1930s under the Franco regime, the cells beneath the building became the site of many human rights' demonstrations. Adjacent to this building was a large, bronze statue that evolved into the symbol of Madrid – a bear reaching for the fruit of a strawberry tree.

The *Puerta del Sol* square was also witness to an uprising against the French in 1808 and the site of the assassination of the prime minister, Jose Canalejas, in 1912. With both Dee and I interested in social studies, we kept our guidebook handy in order not to miss any historical site. Remarkably, I was enjoying Spain more than I thought I would.

I was thoroughly entranced with the *Palacio Real* – the Royal Palace. It was situated on a bluff, and for centuries this site had housed a royal fortress. A fire in 1734 destroyed the fortress, and it was replaced by a magnificent palatial structure – the *Palacio Real*. The interior of the palace was lavishly decorated with ceiling paintings, superb tapestries, marble staircases, and rooms with grand chandeliers and golden statues. The exuberant décor displayed the tastes of many royal families, and the palace was still used for state occasions.

"This palace really reminds me of Versailles," Dee commented as we strolled through the extraordinary rooms, soaking up the incredible Spanish architecture, rich with golden wood and arches.

"Actually, it's even more beautiful, I think. Look at these walls covered in porcelain. The pamphlet says that this green and white porcelain depicting cherubs was kilned in a nearby factory in the early 1700s. It's extraordinary," I commented.

"My favorite has been the banquet room with the huge, long table. Imagine the royal family entertaining in that room," Dee said, stopping with me for a breath of fresh air at a second-floor window looking out onto the gardens.

"Versailles' gardens, though, are hard to beat. The flowers down there are beautiful, but the landscaping in Versailles is more spectacular, don't you think?" I asked.

I turned to find that Dee had disappeared, and I was talking to an elderly Spanish gentleman, who obviously was not bi-lingual. He tipped his hat as I murmured "excuse me" and went in search of Dee, already enthralled with royal tapestries in the next room.

* * * * * * * * *

We walked to the flamenco-dancing event that evening. I had received directions from the hotel clerk and thought that we could easily find the nightclub. Little did I realize how dark, winding, and confusing the streets would be. Although the hotel clerk had said that it was only a five-minute walk, we knew that European walking-time was always deceptive. We walked for perhaps fifteen minutes and still had no clue, and it seemed that the nightclubs were getting sleazier by the minute.

"Dee, I think that we're lost. I don't like this area, and I don't see anything that says 'Eldorado Club.'"

"Well, let's turn around and start back. Maybe we missed it."

Rounding the corner, we both saw the sign at the same time.

"There it is, Dee. Gosh, we must have been blind."

Without hesitating, we opened the door of the club and stepped in. It was dark, but the stage was well lit – with a display of topless lady dancers and more-than-suggestive male dancers. For a split second, our eyes were glued to the stage. Never having been to a strip tease club, we could not in our wildest imaginations envisioned what we saw that night. Brief sequined "strings" of glitter and sparkle made up the entirety of the dancers' costumes. Without a word – we were too stunned to speak – we both turned and bolted through the outside door.

Dee was consumed with laughter, and I merely said, "Wrong place."

It was indeed the right name but obviously the wrong club – or, at least, not what we had expected of flamenco dancers. Stopping a police officer for directions, within the next ten minutes we found the 'Eldorado Club' with the entertainment that we had been seeking.

We spent the next two hours watching the incredible

Spanish flamenco dancers, afire with not only their magnificent talent and but also with their elaborate clothing and instruments.

"I can't believe that these Spanish men and women can create this magical rhythm with just the guitar, castanets, hand clapping, and foot movements. What exciting entertainment," Dee noted, unable to pull her eyes from the colorful-costumed people on stage.

"They are so graceful – fluid, I guess, is a good word. I can't even imagine doing those dance steps with those high heels," I added, mentally calculating the height of the heels. "They must be four inches high."

We both sat in awe, watching the extraordinary talent of the Spanish who were so full of expression and energy.

"This program guide says that gypsies started the dance in the Middle Ages as an artistic expression of the joys and sorrows in life," I said, reading the information given to us at the door. "Do you know that the dancers improvise their movements as they dance, following the rhythm of the guitars? The movements also are dependent on their feelings," I said as I glanced at Dee. "Wow. So they are making these dances up as they go." I pondered that thought for a moment. "You know, I used to have to practice 'step, shuffle, tap' for half and hour just to get it right. I can't imagine getting up and improvising the entire dance."

"That's incredible," Dee remarked. "I love the costumes," she continued. "The long, red and black skirts are beautiful. And I really like the ruffles on the bottom. I used to have a dress with ruffles…"

Dee's voice was drowned out by the harmonious clapping of the dancers as well as of the audience – all in time with the music. An occasional *Ole* resounded from the stage as the dancers whirled and stamped to the mesmerizing sounds of the guitar.

"How remarkable that the Spanish still maintain this traditional event. This is some of the most fantastic entertainment we've seen. Thanks for insisting on coming here, Dee," I said sincerely.

The evening was a thrilling experience, and we returned to the Castillo's apartment by midnight to find the elderly couple sitting on their balcony, candles filling the night air with fragrance of musky rose. We waved to them, and they motioned for us to join them for coffee and chocolate cookies puffed up with air and a light cream.

Empty dishes sat on the small table on the balcony. Typically, the Spanish ate dinner around 11 o'clock at night, so the Castillos had just finished eating as we arrived. Senora disappeared into the kitchen for two more cups and plates and poured steaming Spanish coffee into the demi-cups, already half full of cream.

Because neither spoke English, Dee decided to do her best interpretation of a flamenco dancer in an attempt to demonstrate where we had been. They laughed and clapped, showing they understood, and putting my fingertips to my lips, I threw a kiss into the air, knowing the universal signal meant "superb."

In the candlelight, enhanced by the full moon, we looked at the Castillo's photo album that they had been leafing through when we arrived. A beautiful Spanish girl in her twenties was perched on a tall stool, her black hair falling down her back in ringlets. Her gorgeous white-sequined gown flowed to the floor, ruffles and lace adorning the hem and sleeves. Even with the beautiful gown, the real focal point of the picture was her rich brown, liquid eyes.

The pride in the Castillos' eyes showed that she was either a daughter in younger years or a granddaughter. The next photo cleared up the question as it showed their middle-aged daughter and this lovely granddaughter from the previous picture together on a beach. Dee and I spent an enjoyable half hour looking at family photos. Not knowing who most of the people were didn't matter. The Castillos' pride showed as we looked at their large, handsome family, and we knew they were pleased that we had shared a small part of our evening with them.

* * * * * * * * * *

Dee planned the bullfight event for the following afternoon.

"Enjoy your educational and cultural experience, Dee," I called a bit sarcastically as she left to catch a bus to the arena.

"I will. It'll be great. You'll be sorry you didn't go," she called in a rather pompous, sassy tone.

"Don't think so. I don't want to watch cold-blooded murder. Sorry, did I say murder? Meant slaughter."

I spent two hours at the *Museo del Prado*, which contained some of the world's greatest Spanish paintings. I especially loved Velazquez's collection. *The Triumph of Bacchus* was painted to depict the mythological Bacchus, god of wine. The dark colors, highlighted with a brilliant yellow, reminded me of some of Rembrandt's paintings.

Walking to *Plaza Mayor*, I visited the many unique, quaint shops and cafes of the area. The plaza was picturesque with the balconies, slate roofs, dormer windows, and rounded archways. The square had a theatrical atmosphere and was once used for bullfights, trials by the Inquisition, and executions. Topping off the scenery was an equestrian statue, which dominated the center of the square.

As the afternoon started to wane, I headed back to the Castillo's to see if Dee had returned from the bullfight. I didn't, however, want to hear the gory details of the cruel fight. Entering our room, there was Dee sitting in the chair by the window, and I could tell by the dark look of dismay on her face that something had gone wrong.

"Are you okay, Dee?"

"No, I'm not. Oh, J.J., it was awful!" Dee exploded,

tears streaming down her cheeks.

"Gosh, what happened?" I conjured sympathy in my voice although I was tempted to say, "I told you so."

"Want to talk about it?" I continued cautiously.

I knew that Dee had read that the bull was going to have to die even if was a slow, brutal death; there was no getting around that fact, and I thought that Dee was prepared for that consequence. Apparently not, I thought, as I looked at her eyes, full of anxiety.

"Well, you know that a bus went directly to the *Plaza de Toros* where the bullfight occurred. The crowd was already cheering and clapping when I arrived. Actually, the excitement before the fight was really mesmerizing. At that time, I was still glad to be there." She stopped to catch her breath as she gazed out of the window. She seemed hesitant to continue.

Finally, she looked back at me. "As soon as the actual bullfight started, I knew I couldn't handle it. It was absolutely dreadful – cruel and heartless. I sat with my head down, my eyes jammed shut, and I tried to block out the roar of *Ole*. Of course, no one is allowed to leave in the middle of a fight. It would be very impolite."

"How long does a fight last?"

"It depends. This one lasted twenty minutes because the bull refused to die. Let's not talk about that."

"Okay, go on then," I urged, searching her face for a clue as to what "dreadful" incident had happened, aside from the cruel death of the bull.

"Well, as soon as the first fight was over, I got up to leave. There were six fights in all, but I just wanted out of the arena after the first one." She was still wiping tears from her eyes.

"So you sat through the entire first fight?"

"Well, I sat through it but didn't watch. Anyway, you haven't heard the worst. All the exits of the arena were blocked except one. I thought I could find that one exit, but being confused and upset after that awful fight, I couldn't find it. Finally, I got behind a Spanish couple, who looked as if they knew the way. I just tagged along, praying silently all the time."

"They knew their way?" I questioned.

"I thought so. Boy, was I wrong. We wound around the backside of the arena until we got to a door. It didn't say exit but I thought they knew where they were going. I figured that it would open onto the street. I kept thinking 'fresh air' and followed closely because I wanted out of that god-awful place. J.J., you won't believe this!" Dee was nearly hysterical now.

"What, Dee?" I couldn't imagine what could have been so awful.

"The door opened into a room." Again Dee stopped, seemingly unable to continue.

"A room?" What could be so bad about that, I'm thinking. "Well, go on, Dee," I urged.

"On a large slab in the center of the room was the dead bull, legs sticking straight up. They were hosing him down with…with water!" she gasped, covering her face with her hands, sobs shaking her body.

For a moment I was too dumbfounded to react. There was the memory of Dee saying in her cocky, haughty fashion that the bullfight would be an "educational and cultural experience." Then, there was the image of her standing in the room trying to overcome the unspeakable, dreadful sight of the dead bull, ready for dismemberment. I imagined the floor red with blood and guts, and I shivered at the thought.

"I'm so sorry, Dee," I said genuinely, putting my arms around her shaking body. I knew she had paid a high price for this valued bullfight for which she had yearned.

"Why didn't you talk me out of this stupid idea?" she cried. "I wish I had been a wimp like you." She was still sobbing when she said, "Do you have any tranquilizers because I'll never sleep tonight! The image of the poor, pitiful bull is cemented in my mind – *permanently*," she wailed.

I tried to think what to do or say to support as well as comfort.

Maybe a glass of wine would help," I said, trying to suggest something that would at least temporarily help in settling her nerves.

Eventually, later that evening we went for a glass of wine. At Dee's insistence, however, it had to be white wine; the red reminded her of blood.

It was months before she saw even a speck of the humor in the situation. I was always glad that it was Dee who attained the memorable, never-to-be-forgotten experience that day and not me. I had many other European adventures that helped mold me into a more mature individual by the conclusion of the trip, but that wasn't one of them. That experience was given to Dee alone. Years later, the Spanish bullfight was still a sore subject. Fortunately, I had no authentic pictures to remind me of that event, only a picture of two glasses of white wine.

Chapter 15

All Aboard

At 7 o'clock the next morning with the green giant slung over my shoulder and my brown suitcase being dragged at my side, we arrived at the Madrid train station, ready to endure the long train ride across France into Switzerland. I had exchanged money in the bank the day before, obtaining Swiss francs, but Dee still had Spanish pesedas.

As we got ready to board the train, I suggested, "Dee, we have half an hour before the train leaves. Put your bags on board and go to the currency window and exchange your pesedas. What if it's a Swiss national holiday, and all the banks are closed when we arrive in Switzerland? Remember Germany?"

"You're right," she grinned. "Let's get our luggage onto the train, and you sit guard while I exchange my money."

The train was not unusually crowded. There were five cars going to Switzerland, and we always double-checked the sign on the window to make sure we were on the correct car. We had learned that much on our first train ride – check to see your car's destination. We easily found two seats, situated our suitcases, and Dee returned to the terminal.

Sitting back, I propped my legs over my luggage. Stickers of the Eiffel Tower and the Big Ben stared at me as I closed my eyes, still tired from arising early. Suddenly, I felt the train bolt forward as if hit from behind. Instantly, my eyes flew open, and to my horror, we were beginning to move – slowly at first, but we were indeed moving out of the station. Jumping to the adjacent seat, I viewed the departing train depot through the window.

"Oh, my gosh," I whispered in panic. Dee was nowhere in sight. Meanwhile, the train was picking up speed.

Looking toward the elderly couple in our car, I screamed, "Why are we leaving early?" From their blank expressions, I knew they didn't speak English.

The thought of jumping off the train crossed my mind, but then there was the issue with our bags. I couldn't leave them behind. Bags or Dee – which was more important? Unconsciously, I must have voted on the bags because I remained on the train, even though I was now in a near-manic state.

In a frenzy, I threw open the doors to the attached cars, running through the next four compartments, screaming the same question to the few people on board. "Why are we leaving early?" They either didn't answer or shrugged and said, "I don't know."

Wild thoughts were now flooding my mind – how will I ever find Dee? Why hadn't we decided on a meeting place in case we got separated? I have Dee's luggage so what will she possibly do? My mind was racing – hysteria set in.

By then I had reached a car with half a dozen teenagers. All possessing band instruments, I quickly decided that they must be a part of some organized group. They seemed to be chatting calmly, and I interrupted their conversation as I screamed, "Do you kids know why we are moving?"

Somehow, they seemed to possess some insight as to our early departure.

"Yeah. The train is leaving the depot in order to allow a few cars to be added to it. We'll go back into the station in about ten minutes." He seemed confident.

"How do you know this?" I asked, wanting desperately to believe him. I needed to grasp to some kind of faint hope that I'd see Dee again – this summer – in Europe. "My friend is still in the station exchanging money."

"Because our band leader is still in the station and was told that the train was adding cars," he answered, and another young man nodded in agreement.

I must have looked like a frazzled idiot because one girl

put her arm around my shoulders. "Are you okay?"

"Oh, yeah, thanks." I mustered a faint smile, embarrassed at how crazy I must have seemed. Quickly, I tried to slink out of the car.

Breathing a sigh of relief, I whispered a prayer of thanks and tried to walk casually back through the four cars, hoping no one would recognize me as the insane raving maniac. If only I could fade into the woodwork, I thought, as I took my seat, trying to look as if nothing had happened.

The train had, indeed, slowed down and actually seemed to be coming to a stop. It went forward and backward a few times and then started to return to the station.

Looking out of the window, the first sight I saw as we returned to the depot was Dee standing by the tracks wildly waving her arms over her head. I could read her lips saying, "J.J. J.J." She, too, was in hysterics. I was hoping that the people on the train didn't connect the deranged person sitting on the train with the madwoman waving from the depot.

As the train came to a stop, Dee burst into the car. "Thank, God!" she exclaimed as she grabbed me and placed a genuine kiss on my cheek. "I thought I'd never see you again. I was exchanging my money when I glanced up and saw the train leaving. I started to scream, and the clerk at the exchange booth thought I'd gone crazy. I tried to explain to him that my train was moving out of the station. I just grabbed my money and ran," Dee concluded, wiping the perspiration from her face. "I've never said so many Hail Marys in my life."

I looked around, hoping that the few people in our compartment were not looking. Of course, they had never seen two psychopaths in action, so, naturally, they were watching. I pushed Dee down into her seat, shushing her.

"Talk quietly. The passengers on the train already think I'm nuts," I intervened, "because I was running through the cars, trying to find out why the train was leaving early." I smiled for the first time since the ordeal began, and I, too, collapsed into my seat in a fit of giggles. "I hope that I don't have to see any of those people in the other compartment again."

Dee was cackling, nonstop. "I see the restroom right there between our car and the next one. Going to the bathroom is our only real reason to get up, so you'll never see any of those passengers again," she smiled reassuringly. I knew that in the past few weeks, our luck had never run true-to-course, so already I had my doubts about not seeing the inside of the other four cars.

We decided to transfer our bags into the luggage area at one end of our car. We breathed a deep sigh of relief as we settled down into our well-padded seats, ready for the long haul.

"The train is starting to move, so apparently, we're officially leaving this time," Dee noted, looking out the window.

A conductor had just entered our car and was checking the tickets of the elderly couple near us and the other few passengers who had taken their seats. As he confronted us, he checked our Eurail passes and asked with a thick accent what our destination would be.

"Lucerne, Switzerland," I answered.

"This car is now heading for Paris. You must move forward five cars," he said, pointing to the cars containing the passengers who knew me as the crazy girl – the nut. I began squirming in my seat at the thought of re-visiting those cars.

"Oh, my gosh, Dee. I can't go through those cars again."

"We'll have to unless we want to return to Paris," she replied with a faint smile.

"Do you have anything that I can use in order to go incognito past those people? A large paper bag to put over my head would be fine," I continued, feeling totally embarrassed at the prospect of facing those passengers.

"Well, let's go and get it over," Dee concluded. "Since you have decided that they already think that you're insane, why don't I hold your hand. Then they'll conclude that I'm the caretaker and that you have finally been captured."

"More likely – if you're holding my hand – they'll think you're my accomplice, and we're both insane. Actually, there's a variety of thoughts they could have if you're holding my hand," I laughed in a feeble attempt to muster enough confidence to walk through the compartments.

We gathered our bags, and for the first time, I was really conscious of my neon-green bag and hot pink bow. Trying to look inconspicuous was going to be difficult. Nonchalantly, I tried to stroll through the first car. In the second car, I smiled sheepishly at the elderly Spanish gentleman in the compartment. I had screamed my question at him twice before realizing he spoke no English. Of course, I wasn't sure – maybe he was deaf. I nodded apologetically to a mother and child who looked at me strangely – maybe fearfully – as we continued through the car.

In the third compartment, a stately gentleman was occupying an aisle seat when my plump carry-on caught him on the side of his head, jilting his glasses askew. I attempted an apology, but I was succumbing to embarrassment at many levels by that time. Were people staring at me because of my previous entrance into the car or because of my neon luggage and bright pink accessories? I didn't know.

As we reached the fourth car, unbelievably the snack cart was blocking our way.

"Oh, no, the snack cart! There's no way to get past it, and it's moving at a snail's pace. Of course, everyone in this car will get a really good look at me again," I whispered to Dee, who was snickering.

For five minutes we stood behind the snack cart with a

man serving coffee and rolls. He kept glaring at us as we stood behind him, and every once in a while, Dee would accidentally bump him with her elephantine bag. "Sorry," I'd hear her mutter.

"Obviously, that guy in charge of the cart is disturbed with us because we want to pass," Dee noticed. "He's giving us the 'evil eye' because I slightly touched him a few times with my bag."

"Like it was our idea to change cars," I whispered. "I'd be happy to crawl under one of these seats and bury myself. These passengers are all looking at me." I felt like a person with three heads – a real freak.

"It's your imagination, J.J."

"No, Dee, it's not. That little boy…that little three-year-old boy who is harmless and innocent even knows that I'm stupid. He was pointing at me and laughing. I'm a moron to these people," I whispered.

Just then Dee's bags were snatched up and heaved over the cart. Her newly bought sword for her brother – delicately placed in a side pocket – flew over the top of the suitcase, clanging loudly as it hit the aisle.

I looked up to see a flash of green being catapulted into the air, listening to a resounding "thud" as it landed on the other side. The pink-beribboned one was more difficult to hurl, and it knocked two bottles of Coke off the cart before it landed with a plop out of sight. The man operating the cart glared at us one final time before ridding himself of us permanently.

"Well, thank you, sir," I said sarcastically. Still, I tried to smile pleasantly as we squeezed through the three-inch space between the seats and the cart.

I attempted a polite nod to the passenger who was nearly stabbed with Dee's sword, trying to make him believe that we were the victims of this "madman's" temper.

"He shouldn't be working the cart if he can't control his temper," I whispered to another passenger who, too, had barely escaped injury from the flying weapon. I knew that he didn't speak English, but it didn't matter.

Grabbing our bags, Dee nonchalantly tried to slide her sword back into the side pocket, and we scrambled out of the car as quickly as possible. We made our way to the next car, which was bound for Lucerne. To my relief, I didn't recognize any passengers in the compartment.

"Thank goodness," I said, sinking into a seat. "No one in here has seen me."

Dee was laughing hysterically by now as she, too, collapsed into a seat. "Okay, this has been a crazy day already, and it's only just begun. What else can happen?" she asked.

"Don't know but we're going to be on this train until late tonight," I concluded.

* * * * * * * * *

The scenery throughout northern Spain was sensational. It was a bright day. There was not a cloud in the sky, and we enjoyed everything – the rugged mountainous terrain, tiny, ancient villages, endless grape vineyards crawling up the hillsides, and castles perched high in the Spanish mountains.

Again, we decided to stop at unforeseen villages in Spain and France, stretching our time to three days before reaching the French Alps, which were far more spectacular than we had ever imagined. The countryside was gorgeous with breathtaking mountain peaks and sparkling, crystal-blue lakes. Many of the jagged mountaintops were snow-covered, brilliantly glistening in the late afternoon sun. The magnificent panorama continued to unfold, and we saw the most spectacular scenery of the trip. Long after dark – four days after leaving Madrid – we finally arrived at our destination – the beautiful and historic city of Lucerne, Switzerland.

Chapter 16

Alpine Splendor

The train station was centrally located so we had no trouble finding lodging in a small Swiss hotel, situated on the edge of Lake Lucerne. We couldn't see the Alps at night, but we knew they were surrounding us and could hardly wait until morning to soak up the Alpine splendor.

We sauntered to a nearby café for a light, evening meal of cold, sliced vegetables with salad dressing. Cooked green beans, corn, carrots, tomatoes, olives, and zucchini with parsley delicately placed along the edges of the plate was a European specialty, called *Gemuse Schussell*. A plate of various Swiss chesses completed the meal. We ordered a glass of the house wine – red, dry, and smooth – always a compliment to any European meal. Reluctantly, Dee had a glass of the red wine even though she had sworn it off in Madrid.

Now being used to the long, leisurely European meal schedule, we sat, ate, and chatted. A group of high school students arrived during our three-hour meal. They were escorted by several teachers and were on a ten-day tour of France, Switzerland, Austria, and Italy. We quickly joined into their lively conversation, being desperate to hear American language spoken – no accents or explaining the meaning of a word. Just good old American talk. The group was from St. Louis, so we felt as if we were kindred spirits from the Midwest. Being on their last night in Lucerne, they were heading for Austria in the morning.

Our table sat directly behind Stacey and Jenny, who were obviously great friends, and from their conversation, they seemed especially mature for their seventeen years. They were petite and bubbly and could have passed for sisters, both possessing endearing smiles and blue eyes. They were interested in having fun but really considered the trip as a learning tool, thinking that one day they wanted to be foreign language teachers – Jenny, French and Stacey, German – and hoped that this experience abroad would help them make that final decision.

Jenny's love of France had originated from having a French foreign exchange student live with her family for a year. Claudette brought to Jenny's family all the warmth and sophistication that often is found in an intimate friendship with a young, French person. The previous year, Jenny had visited the Alsace-Lorraine area of France where Claudette lived, and this year, Jenny decided to spread her wings to other countries by joining the high school cultural studies class on their tour, which included France, Switzerland, Germany, and Austria.

Stacey's grandparents had been born in Austria – thus, her interest in the German language. The next city on their tour would be Innsbruck, Austria. Igls, a village outside of Innsbruck, was the birthplace of her grandmother, and Stacey could hardly wait to visit the little town tucked away in the Alps.

We exchanged addresses, and Stacey wrote me later that year to express her fascination with Igls. When she saw the spectacular snow-capped Alps and the quaint old-world village with such Austrian charm, she felt as if she had visited that beautiful resort area in some other place or time. She wanted to return and did her junior year in college, taking a German course through an exchange program.

That was the summer of 1976, and Stacey found in that village the love-of-her-life – a young German instructor followed her back to America to ask for her hand in marriage. The last letter I received from Stacey, she and Ludwig still lived in Igls with three additions to their family.

At 10 o'clock we bid the high school group goodnight – spending a full ten minutes just saying goodbye to Jenny and Stacey – as we headed across town to our hotel. We fell into bed after the long, adventurous day.

"What fun talking to Jenny and Stacey. They were so mature for their age. Even though we were older, I wonder it we were that pulled together on last year's trip?" Dee grinned as she reached to turn off the light.

"Yeah, I was thinking the same thing, Dee. They were great kids," I commented with a yawn, pulling the soft comforter tighter around my shoulders. "I don't think that even now we're that mature," I commented with a grin.

"Umm" was her only comment.

It was quiet for a while, and I thought that Dee had drifted off to sleep when she said, groggily, "That was quite an adventure today."

Innocently, I asked, "Oh, you mean the train?"

"Yeah," she giggled. "You know, I don't think I've ever been left anyplace before. You'd think that with fourteen kids, my parents would have miscounted once in a while," Dee laughed. "However, it had to be on another continent that I got lost."

"I remember that I dreamed one time when I was little that my mom had left me in the grocery store. I woke up screaming. It was so real," I said, almost trembling, just thinking of that dream. "It took days for me to realize that my mom wouldn't have left me anywhere, and that it was truly just a dream."

"It would be hard to forget you – you were the only child."

"Actually, it would have been easy to forget me because I was so quiet that you'd not even know that I was around," I smiled, thinking of my early childhood when I truly was extremely shy and bashful. How things had changed, I thought.

I glanced over at Dee, who was surprisingly silent – a

soft snore escaped from her mouth as she lay snuggled under the down comforter.

* * * * * * * * * *

Arising early the next morning, we went directly to our small, open balcony to get our first glimpse of the exquisite Swiss Alps, which surrounded Lucerne. White clouds hung low over the alpine peaks, but we could see summits of the mountains stretching high into the billowy sky. Beneath the clouds and fog, we could see streaks of snow on the sides of the mountains. The tops were probably snow capped, but they wouldn't be visible until later in the day when the fog lifted and the sun glistened through.

"You know what would be fun?" Dee asked. "Going up into the Alps and staying in a village."

"That's a great idea," I added. "Let's see if we can catch a train into the mountains tonight."

We spent the morning strolling through the narrow, winding, cobblestone streets and alleys of Old Lucerne, stopping in the numerous shops and boutiques. Lunch was wonderful at a little sidewalk cafe located on the edge of beautiful, blue Lake Lucerne, and we watched the ducks and swans feeding off the morsels of food thrown into the water by the diners.

The Chapel Bridge, built in 1333, spanned the width of Lake Lucerne and was ornately decorated with gable paintings that glorified the heroic deeds of the city's early Christians. Old but still sturdy, the bridge had made it possible for millions of tourists to cross the span of Lake Lucerne and view both sides of the beautiful city. Years after we visited Lucerne, the bridge burned completely but was miraculously reconstructed exactly as the original one.

The Lion Monument, which was carved in 1820 to eulogize the Swiss heroes from the 1792 war with France, had become a most famous icon of Lucerne. Situated in the

176

side of a mountain, busloads of tourists streamed into the alcove each year to see the celebrated lion.

"I love this city," Dee said as we strolled back to the hotel.

"You love every city, Dee," I commented with a smile.

"Yes, but there's so much history here," she noted.

"And beauty," I added.

"Yes, of course, beauty. Everywhere you look, it's gorgeous."

It was early afternoon when we arrived back at the hotel. Having made the decision to move to an Alpine village for the night, we only needed to pick up our luggage and check out. Fortunately, we hadn't unpacked from our arrival the night before.

I had started several days earlier to stuff my dirty clothes down onto the bottom of my suitcase, and everything was a jumbled mess. Nothing was folded anymore – everything was wadded and wrinkled. Glancing at Dee's suitcase, it was still neatly packed. How can this be, I wondered. I'm the organized one, and normally Dee is in complete disarray.

However, this time my suitcase was crammed with a pile of clothes, which resembled something that my dog would adore – a mess that she could bury her nose in, digging and scattering everything to and fro before curling herself into a ball to sleep. Quickly, I slammed the suitcase shut on the disheveled hodgepodge, and we headed directly for the train station to find transportation to an alpine village.

The depot was old and quaint with wooden benches in rows through the center of the small room. Several ticket booths lined the side of the depot with only one in use.

"Der ist a 3 o'clock train going to Engelberg," the small, gray-haired man, who was selling tickets and sporting the traditional dress of *lederhosen,* replied to our inquiry. "Dat village ist in de middle of de Alps. From der,

177

you can catch a cog train to Mount Titlus, which ist 10,000 meters high," he said, talking and counting the tickets at the same time as he looked through his small, wire-rimmed spectacles.

"Perfect!" Dee exclaimed.

We bought two tickets, and at 3 o'clock we had boarded the train bound for Engelberg.

What a spectacular view we experienced on our way to that Alpine village – lush green pastures with grazing, brown Swiss cattle, mountain goats in combat on the cliffs, Alpine houses spaced intermittently in the valleys, steep, clear waterfalls spilling down the sides of the Alps, and snow – white and glistening – covering the highest mountain pinnacles. I sat on the edge of my seat, snapping pictures – one after another – through the train window.

As our train entered Engelberg, we spotted a small hotel, built in Swiss chalet fashion.

"Let's see if there's vacancy in that hotel, J.J. It's close plus it's so…well, so Swiss looking."

Indeed, there was a vacancy on the first floor, the price was right, and our balcony – with a window box stuffed full of bright red geraniums – looked out onto the incredible sight of Mount Titlus.

As we unpacked a few necessities, Dee had a suggestion. "I saw a grocery store down the street. How about buying food for dinner tonight and eating on our balcony."

"Okay, great idea," I agreed, brushing my hair back into a ponytail. I applied some lipstick, washed my hands, and looked at Dee who was staring out the window at the Alpine view. Dense networks of lifts covered one side of a distant mountain, superb for skiing. A touch of winter wonderland awaited the ski tourists, ascending into the higher Alps.

"Let's hit the streets of Engelberg and find that grocery store," I smiled as Dee turned and nodded.

We sauntered down the small, cobblestone main street

of the village. Lights in some of the shops were flickering on as clouds started to cover the mountain sun. We found the small, neighborhood grocery, and as we entered, the sight and smell of the fresh, juicy fruit stopped us – oranges, apples, bananas, strawberries and cherries.

"I've been hungry for oranges," I commented, my mouth watering at the prospect. Starting to pick up the orange, the clerk snapped at me in German.

I looked at Dee who was smiling. "I think he doesn't want you to touch the fruit. You better just point at what you want."

Pointing first to the oranges and then to the apples – holding up two fingers all the while – he nodded and seemed pleased with my decision not to touch the fruit.

"Must be a European custom. I've been scolded before for touching the fruit. I don't understand how I can possibly destroy or mangle an orange by touching it," I commented.

I remembered an experience in Paris the previous year when I was berated for touching the peaches. A slew of French words flew from the grocer's mouth as I picked up the fruit to see if it was ripe. He scared me so much that I dropped the fresh peach and received a still harsher reprimand. Quickly, I reached into my purse to pay for the peach that lay splattered on the ground, but the grocer waved his hand at me as he rounded the counter to clean it up.

Dee was silent as she eyed the cherries, which were her favorite fruit. After I had paid for my fruit, the clerk turned to her.

"Cherries," she said, having learned from my mistakes that she must only point.

The clerk, obviously limited in his English, asked, "Half a kilo? Kilo?"

Not knowing the European measurements, Dee gave him a blank look. "Well, I love cherries." She turned to look at me, hoping I would give her some advice. When I didn't, she replied, "A kilo."

Not knowing too much about European measurements, I *did* know that a kilo was more than she wanted. However, I decided not to stop her, as I wanted to see her face when she received a full kilo. Dee's eyes began to widen as she watched the clerk scoop and scoop and scoop the cherries into the bag. I was laughing by now.

"Did you know how much a kilo was?" she whispered as she paid the clerk, suspecting that I had let her buy five times the amount she could possibly eat.

"I had a idea, but I thought we needed a good laugh. Together, we should be able to carry them to the hotel room."

"Smart-aleck," she smirked. "Well, they're a great laxative," she commented as she grabbed the huge bag, heaped with succulent, juicy, red cherries.

Arriving back at the hotel, we carefully unpacked our delicious, healthy dinner. As we ate the tasty Swiss cheese, bread, yogurt, and fruit – which consisted of lots of cherries – we made plans for the next day. We decided to go to Mount Titlus in the afternoon and then leave the following morning on the train for Italy. We had learned our lesson with trains – no more night trains for us, only day trains.

* * * * * * * * * * *

Lying in bed the next morning, half asleep, I was awakened at 6:30 with a tremendous echoing of horns – alpine horns.

"Dee, wake up! Listen to that. I think it's alpine horns. The sound must be bouncing off the mountains and reverberating. Wow, this is fantastic."

"Gosh, J.J., what time is it?" Dee asked, not nearly as impressed with the deep, bellowing, bass echo of the horns as I was.

"It's 6:30," I said, checking my watch. "I've got to get

dressed and see those horns. I'll bet the men blowing the horns are dressed in their traditional Swiss costumes, just waiting to pose for a Kodak moment." I heard a snicker from under the covers, but no movement followed. I was dressed and out the door in five minutes.

Dee was up and dressed when I returned at 7:45.

I tried to describe to her what I had seen; however, words just didn't do the experience justice. Huge, curved horns – decorated with intricate paintings of folklore and Alpine flowers – bellowed out the deep tones to the morning Alps. The baritone, stereophonic celebration of echoes reverberated off the sides of the mountains, touching the very soul of every listener. Men dressed in their traditional lederhosen, Swiss hats with Edelweiss, long stockings, and hiking shoes tenderly held the magnificent horns that looked as if they had been originally carved for the giants of the mountains – so immense was the size.

Walking back to the hotel, I encountered the Swiss farmers on their early trek to the pastures with their sheep and goats. Together they strolled through the village streets, Swiss cowbells jingling and clanging in time to the animals' saunter. Watching the farmers with their long staffs corralling their livestock into some sort of a line as they performed their daily meander through the village caused me to scramble for my camera to capture the moment so familiar to this tiny Swiss town.

"You know, Dee," I said with a twinkle, "There are so many different designs on the cow bells that I'll bet you could get 13 for your siblings and not one would be alike." I waited for Dee's reply. There was none – only a glance out of the corner of her eye.

"Well, just so you know – I bought one for myself to put onto my carry-on. It's not always easy to see my green bag," I remarked dryly, "and I thought a Swiss cow bell would be of great assistance if I lost it."

Dee's giggle was her only response as she picked up

my newly purchased bell to examine it. The three-inch, bronze bell, topped with red and blue material and embroidered white Edelweiss flowers, would hang perfectly from the green handle on my bag.

"Seriously, though, this village is so quaint – I love it. Oh, by the way, did I mention that today is a Swiss national holiday?" I continued casually.

"You've got to be kidding! These holidays are following us all over Europe." Dee, who was applying her makeup, glanced over her shoulder at me. "Hey, are the banks open?" Fear sounded in Dee's voice.

"Probably not. It's too early to know," I replied. "Thank goodness you got your money exchanged in Spain. I guess our traumatic train experience and my act of insanity were not in vane," I chuckled. "Anyway, there's a big festival tonight – a parade, band, and traditional costumes."

"Sounds like fun. By the way, the train going to Mount Titlus isn't shut down in celebration of the national holiday, is it?" Dee questioned.

"No, I checked on that. A cog train goes up every hour."

Whatever we had read about the magnificent scenery of the Alps couldn't have prepared us for that trip. The splendor of the mountain terrain was awesome. We ascended the green-covered hills used for grazing the cows – harnessed with Swiss cowbells – and passed the rustling lush Alpine grasses, which soon gave way to dense timberland. The higher we got, the taller the trees became. First were evergreens and poplars – branches sprinkled with snow – and then came the majestic white birch, reaching for the cloudless sky. The deep, rocky gorges, jagged crags, and steep, jutting mountaintops added to the breathtaking beauty of the high Alps.

As we neared the top, we looked down and saw valleys cut deep into the heart of some of the highest pinnacles. Engelberg sprawled below us, resting between Alpine peaks, and a chasm-spanning bridge sprung up as we reached a plateau. A group of afternoon daredevils flocked to the cliffs to risk their lives climbing the sides of the mountains, and soon the skies were filled with blue, yellow, and red hang-gliders, floating effortlessly to the solid earth so far below. A white country church – its steeple reaching for the ethereal sky far above the boundless Alps – nestled itself on a green-sided mountain. A few waterfalls descended the mountain as we ascended. Nearing the summit, feathery snow filled the air, adding to the already white rocky terrain. The few trees that withstood the high altitude seemed to be dipped in white chocolate as the flakes clung to every branch and leaf. It was nothing short of celestial beauty.

"Have you ever seen so much pure, white snow in your entire life?" I asked. "I can't even find words to express what I'm seeing – or feeling."

I looked at Dee who remained silent, surveying the distant mountaintops. It was easy to be speechless in beauty that surpassed words.

After staring into the pure, white scenery for a while, I understood what people meant when they talked of "snow blindness." I actually seemed to lose my eyesight – even when I closed my eyes, all I saw was white.

An hour was spent in that paradise – looking over the mountains, which were all so white that they blended together in a fabulously monotonous state. As we stood in the snow – glistening in the sunlight – an occasional rabbit or white-tailed deer came into view and colorful birds perched in the trees, but there was absolutely no sign that urban areas or even human life existed on earth. We felt as if we were part of nature at its best – the purest, whitest fantasy imaginable, and the feeling of "being at one with nature" consumed me.

I remembered this feeling of "oneness" only once before. I was in Madura Canyon outside of Tucson. There was no snow, but the green valleys and cold mountain streams made me realize that God created all of nature to flow together and that I was part of that intricate plan. It wasn't quite the feeling I had in Switzerland, but it was close. That day God was around, above, and within me – it was a moment that I often pondered later in life. Times like those always reaffirmed my faith that God would never forsake us. His prominence seemed bigger than life, though, that day in the Swiss Alps.

Reluctantly by late afternoon, we knew that we had to leave our fantasy world, and at 4 o'clock, we boarded the train to return to civilization.

"Never have I seen anything more beautiful than the mountains, totally covered in pure, white snow," Dee commented during the descending train ride. "It was absolutely awesome."

"I don't think that I've ever seen anything more gorgeous. We'll never be able to describe this to anyone," I commented, reluctant to leave Mt. Titlus, and silently I promised myself that I'd someday return.

We were both quiet on the return trip, soaking up the last bit of unbelievable scenery of the high Alps as we watched the snow-covered ground give way to the green, lush mountainside pastures.

Chapter 17

Final Swiss Memories

That night at 10 o'clock – because it was a Swiss national holiday – the town square was the center of a festive street dance. However, simply *gathering* in the town center was not traditional for the gala event. The townspeople needed to *parade* through the main street leading to the center of the village. The one winding main street was lined with glowing lanterns to light the way, and people carried flaming torches, adding enchantment to the nocturnal scene. A band made up entirely of locals churned out Swiss folk music with their trumpets, accordions, drums, and trombones. Festively, the raucous crowd made their way to the square.

The townswomen were entirely bedecked in long, colorful dresses called *dirndlkleid*. Handmade lace trimmed the puffed sleeves and hems, and intricately laced hats topped off their traditional stylish attire. The men wore olive-green short leather pants – *lederhosen* – knee-length socks, and small hats with feathers. They all sang, clapped, and cheered as they paraded down the street, eventually bolting into the town square. A quartet of men with accordions broke away from the local band to provide Swiss polka music as the party continued with gala dancing in the square.

For perhaps an hour, we watched the frolicking townsfolk from an outdoor café table as the crowd grew more and more boisterous with the flow of drink. As it neared midnight, we grew tired after a long day and decided to call it a night.

Making our way back to the hotel, we could still hear the quartet, belting out wonderful Swiss and German polkas. Even from our balcony, we could see the festivities, which lasted long past midnight.

"Actually, it's more fun up here because we have a panoramic view," Dee noted, hanging out over the balcony rail.

I sat on the balcony with Dee for perhaps half an hour, discussing the beauty we had seen that day – splendor that had surpassed everything either of us had ever experienced in our lives. We knew we could never describe the Alps to anyone, nor would pictures do the magnificent mountains justice. We would have to return home with memories cemented into our minds of the incredible Swiss Alps and the spectacular white paradise we had had the privilege of seeing that day.

Eventually, I grew restless and decided to rummage through my brown suitcase, rearranging my mess.

"I think I'll discard some of my old t-shirts. I have enough new, clean shirts without the old ones, and I had planned on leaving some of the clothes behind," I remarked, looking at the chaos impacting my luggage. "My clothes are in such a mess, and yours are still neatly packed. I don't know how you did that."

"It's habit. I'm just used to keeping three of my sisters' drawers straightened at home to help my mom."

Once again, I wished I could be a part of a large family, even though it meant more work and responsibility on my part. I hated being the only child. Even though Dee complained at times about her household, which she lovingly named "the zoo," I knew that she loved the large Italian camaraderie of fourteen children.

"Maybe, I'll sort through my luggage, too, and get rid of some of my clothes. We have only one more country, and you had a great idea of bringing some old clothes and leaving them behind, making room for souvenirs," Dee added. "I thought your idea was a little crazy back in the States, but now I'm glad I did it."

We both started to toss out a few shirts and underwear that we thought we wouldn't use. As we rummaged through our bags, Dee pulled out two little Alpine sweaters that she had purchased for her sisters. White snowflakes covered a red sweater and a blue one.

"They're adorable, Dee. Who are they for?"

"Rose and Liz. They'll love them, I think," she said, folding them and replacing them in her bag.

My brown suitcase didn't seem any lighter, and my green carry-on became chubbier than ever as I carefully rearranged breakable souvenirs into it. After another long, eventful day, we decided to retire so that we could catch an early train to Italy.

* * * * * * * * * *

The next morning, the bright, mountain sun was just coming though the window when we crawled out of bed.

"What a beautiful day, " I remarked, stretching as I stood on the balcony, looking at the debris in the street after the night's festivities. I tried to absorb the Alpine view for the last time. There were no clouds and the multiple summits sparkled with glistening snow.

Dee's voice interrupted my thoughts. "May I use the hairdryer first, J.J., while you shower?"

"Sure, be my guest."

I went down the hall to the shower and had just turned on the water when the lights went out.

Ummm, this is strange, I thought.

I quickly finished washing the soap off and grabbed a towel. As I made my way down the hall, I noticed the entire floor was dark. Entering the room, I saw Dee was sitting on the bed, hairdryer in hand.

"I think I may have blown a fuse in the room," Dee said sheepishly, a bit upset with herself. "I forgot that when I'm in Europe that I need to put the hairdryer on low heat instead of high so that there is no surge of electricity."

"Dee, it's not just *our* room. It's the entire floor," I confided to her.

"Oh, no, really?" She ran to the door to peek out. "Oh, my gosh. I can't believe that I did that."

She quickly closed the door, burying her head in the pillow she held in her hand. "I'm really embarrassed," she said, but she was already seeing the light side of the situation as I heard her giggling softly.

The black-out cost us half an hour in time as the manager obviously had trouble locating the correct fuses. We heard him scramble down the hall several times with two housekeepers close at his feet. They chattered in German, trying to decipher not only the origin of the problem but also the extent of the damage. A whole floor without lights was a disaster for the small hotel.

Guests peered from their rooms – half dressed or in their pajamas – all asking questions at once. The manager seemed to be apologizing for the inconvenient situation as he bustled about, trying to rectify the unfortunate disturbance as quickly as possible. Dee felt lucky that she was not discovered to be the culprit who had created total chaos throughout the floor.

Eventually, as the lights finally flickered on, we went to the breakfast room to eat a hurried breakfast – all the time Dee hoping that no one would ask her about the fuse.

"Dee, quit worrying. A fuse went out. There's no way to know that you were the one to cause a floor full of people to be stranded in the dark," I said with a smug grin. "Only a few people missed their train or important meeting. Don't worry about it," I said sarcastically, but all in fun. Dee moaned and tried to muster a faint smile.

For the first time in weeks, I found eggs at the breakfast buffet. Leery of trying any, I felt them to see if they were warm.

"Umm," I said more to myself than Dee.

"What?" she asked, seeing me hesitate, scrutinizing the eggs.

"Trying to decide if they are cooked or raw," I commented.

"I think that it's just Germans that like the raw ones," she said as she put a freshly-baked bun onto her plate.

"I don't know, Dee. They speak some form of German here. The Germans could have corrupted them into believing that the raw-egg fetish is healthy. I think that I'm going to pass even though I'm starving for a boiled egg."

"Here, give me one. I'll be the one who cracks it," she said, grabbing the egg.

Loading our plates with buns, Swiss cheese and yogurt, we both took fruit as well to pocket for a mid-morning snack. Now if the eggs were cooked, they would be a fine addition to the fruit.

I awaited the moment that Dee cracked the egg. It was hard boiled, and I rejoiced by returning to the buffet to get three of them for later in the day.

We returned to our room, and throwing our old, discarded clothes into the corner, we took our suitcases to the lobby.

"You know, my luggage does seem lighter," Dee remarked as we reached the reception desk.

"Mine is just as heavy as ever but maybe not quite as fat," I concluded as the manager looked around the corner.

"Excuse me, sir, may we leave our luggage in the corner until we check the train schedule at the station?"

"Of course, miss," the manager answered, his hair in disarray and his jacket tossed on a nearby chair – probably, discarded in his haste to rectify the electrical problem.

"Why do you want to leave the luggage, J.J.?"

"Well, I was just thinking – if the train doesn't leave for an hour or two, then we'll have to sit in the station and guard the suitcases. If the luggage is here in the hotel, we can window shop in town and then pick them up when we're ready to leave," I replied.

"Brilliant idea."

Dee's luggage now sported a few brightly-colored, glossy travel stickers. I was sure she had been jealous of my unique array of pictures, and I noticed her buying a few in the stationery store on the previous day. Glossy stickers of Mt. Titlus, skiing boots, and "I Love Switzerland" adorned one side of her carry-on.

I had found a key chain bearing a Saint Bernard dog, which I added to the other handle of my carry-on. Saint Bernards were the most honored dogs of the Alps, always the first at a rescue site of an avalanche. I loved dogs and thought it was a suitable addition to my collectibles.

Our train left in forty-five minutes, so we sauntered through the village one last time, peering into shop windows and snapping our last photos of the Alpine splendor. We then stopped at the hotel to get our luggage. There on top of my green carry-on were our discarded clothes, all stacked and neatly folded.

"Oh, my gosh. Our throw-away clothes! I think that the maids thought we forgot them," I laughed. "You know, I read of an American lady traveling in Yugoslavia a few years ago. She had the same idea that we had – pack old clothes and leave them behind. When she returned home, a package arrived from Yugoslavia. It was her old clothes, laundered, ironed, and folded."

Dee chuckled.

Timidly, I turned to the hotel manager, "Sir, we want to throw these clothes away."

"Really, miss? The maid thought you forgot them," the manager answered, still looking a bit disheveled from the earlier fiasco. His hair was combed, but his jacket still lay in a heap on the chair.

Suddenly, the impact of our American wastefulness hit me, and I felt embarrassed. The frugality of the Europeans seemed preferable next to the extravagance of some Americans, who at times thoughtlessly and carelessly wallowed in materialism. I felt ashamed that sometimes our ethics allowed us to be so wasteful in a world in which even food was sometimes a luxury.

In future years, I often thought of that incident as I attempted to teach my own children the value of a dollar and the respect of being fugal in a world – especially America – too absorbed in materialism.

Chapter 18

We caught the 10:30 morning train heading to Venice, Italy. Once again we didn't make it to our destination. Signs for Verona appeared on the landscape.

"Verona! Dee, that's the home of Romeo and Juliet. I *have* to visit Verona," I said, tugging at her sleeve as I pointed to the sign.

"Come on, J.J. *Romeo and Juliet* is a made-up play."

"No, Dee, Shakespeare based the play on real feuding families in Verona."

"Are you sure? I think that it's all a myth or legend, maybe," Dee continued.

"No, Dee. It's a true story. You should have stuck with me through the Shakespeare courses. I would have taught you so much," I grinned.

"So *Romeo and Juliet* is a true story?"

I nodded.

"Well, okay let's visit Verona then," she said, already pulling her carry-on down from the rack above our heads. "It might be fun."

Verona, second largest city in the Veneto region after Venice, is one of the most prosperous cities in northern Italy. The ancient center of Verona contains magnificent ruins, second only to those found in Rome. Medieval rulers built the splendid *palazzi* – constructed of local pink-tinged limestone – in the midst of Verona. Two special focal points are the massive first-century *Arena*, the amphitheater that still maintains current events in the city, and *Piazza Erbe*, the plaza which attracts the local, colorful market.

We spent two delightful days in Verona. I took a roll of film not only of Juliet's home, but also of Romeo's tomb. I found a book in English that explained in detail the tragic story of Romeo and Juliet. The original story was researched by Lungi da Porto of Vicenza in the 1520s and has since inspired countless poems, films, ballets, and dramas. Juliet's house, or *Casa di Giulietta* as it is known in Italian, No. 27 Via Cappello, daily saw throngs of people, who wanted to stand on the small marble balcony and touch the golden statue of Juliet, which Lord Montague erected in tribute to his daughter-in-law.

"Go stand on the balcony, J.J., and I'll take your picture," Dee remarked, pointing to the legendary spot where Juliet dreams of her Romeo, met only hours before at the ball.

I paid the fee – several thousand lira which was actually equivalent to about a dollar – to enter the house and climb the stone stairs. No furniture was left in the house, only a bust of William Shakespeare confronted the tourists at the front door.

"The balcony is so much smaller than I imaged," I concluded, calling down to Dee in the courtyard below. "It's only the width of one window. The movie depicts it as quite huge and elaborate."

Dee quickly snapped a picture of me as I portrayed Juliet in a mock scene, spieling, "Romeo, Romeo, wherefore art thou, Romeo."

* * * * * * * * *

The second – and last – afternoon that we were in Verona, we meandered through the cobblestone streets where the open market sold Italian wares of leather, jewelry, and shoes. Taking time to walk on the top row of the *Arena*, we had a wonderful view of all of Verona, laid out in the midst of one of Italy's lush valleys. We strolled through one of Italy's finest Renaissance gardens, *Giardino Giusti*, laid out in 1580. The formal gardens consist of geometrically-clipped hedges, gravel walks, and red and white potted plants, directly contrasting to the woods and forest at its edge. It has been said by some that this is the finest garden in all of Europe.

And then we sat by one of the beautiful spraying fountains, watching the pigeons gorging themselves on food thrown to them by the tourists. Here, we met Lorenzo, the four-year-old little boy with the huge black eyes that literally talked. He was with his nanny who spoke no English, but language wasn't necessary with Lorenzo.

He meticulously fed the birds that seemed to recognize him from daily visits. They clamored around his feet as he picked his favorites to feed. Removing his sandals, he sat by the flowing fountain, feet dangling and splashing, glees of laughter filling the air. Occasionally, his big liquid eyes would focus on us, and he'd smile and whisper something to his nanny who would look at us and grin.

Before Lorenzo left, I took the ball cap – saved for the really hot, sunny afternoons or for "bad hair days" – that I had in my bag and motioned for him. He said something to this nanny and then strolled over to examine the cap. I carefully placed it on his head, his face a beam of smiles. He crawled up onto the park bench, and reaching for my face with his tiny hands, he placed a quick kiss on my cheek. "*Grazie*," he whispered, his eyes sparkling. He clamored down from the bench to return to his nanny and turned as he walked away, throwing his tiny hand into the air with a wave.

We had thoroughly enjoyed our sojourn to Verona, and Lorenzo was definitely one of the highlights. However, early the next morning, we went to the depot and boarded a train heading for Venice. As we traipsed into the car heading east, we quickly found empty seats, and Dee sleepily laid her head back on her rolled-up jacket.

"I've always dreamed of visiting Venice," she remarked. "I can't wait."

"From what I've read, Venice is one of Europe's most beautiful cities. But, you know, it is slowly sinking into the Adriatic Sea."

"Really?" Dee asked curiously. "What else do you know about Venice?"

"Well, originally, Venice used the water surrounding it as protection from barbarians. The Venetian houses had to be built on poles similar to Amsterdam's houses to protect them from tidal waves and huge storms. However, slowly Venice is losing its battle with the storms and floods."

"How do you know all of this, J.J.?" Dee asked, surprised at my knowledge of so many particulars.

"I read it in *Europe on Five Dollars a Day*," I smiled.

"Get real. You did not," she retorted.

"Actually, I did read some of it in the tour book, but most of the information came from a research paper I did in college about cities that are slowly sinking, both in America and Europe. But I understand that Venice is extremely beautiful," I replied. "Very romantic, too. Maybe you'll find an Italian man-of-your-dreams, Dee."

Dee glanced at me with a smirk, turning her sight back to the train window, revealing the last of the Alpine splendor.

Late afternoon, we arrived at the crowded Venice train station. The depot was in the middle of town, so we grabbed our suitcases and walked toward the nearby hotel district.

My brown luggage seemed a little lighter. Most of the breakable objects had been transferred into my carry-on, which was taking on a new look. Bulging, fat, and out-of-control with newly purchased souvenirs from Verona, it had lost most of its "greenness" to new stickers depicting Romeo, Juliet, Mercutio, and Nurse. They were covering the lower end of the bag, making it more multi-colored than green. And now in addition to the hot pink ribbon, Swiss cowbell, and St. Bernard key chain all adorning the handle,

I had purchased a clove of fresh garlic at the open market. "It'll ward off evil," I was told by the local merchant. Actually, if you got close enough, it warded off *everyone*. The young man selling me the fragrant relic provided a small string bag, which I slipped around the clove and through the bag's handle.

We found a small hotel not far from the station. A handsome, dark Italian hotel clerk greeted us in his limited English. He had a room, and we asked to see it.

We asked if we could leave our suitcases in the lobby as the hotel clerk glanced at my mottled array of European sites plastered topsy-turvy on what used to resemble a carry-on. He agreed, and we climbed the three flights of stairs to the room. After looking at it, we decided to take it even though it was small and more expensive than we had hoped. However, we were tired and our luggage was unbelievably heavy, and we simply didn't want to go in search of another hotel.

Going back for our luggage, we found once again that elevators probably had not been invented when the hotel was constructed. Mentally conditioning ourselves for the long haul, we looked first at the luggage and then at the steep staircase. This time I decided to make two trips, being exhausted from maneuvering two tons of luggage at once up the stairs. Fifteen minutes later, we dropped our bags into the room and left immediately to explore the incredible city of canals, bridges, and gondolas.

We walked toward the famous Rialto Bridge. Before reaching the bridge – Venice's most famous sight, which offers views of the Grand Canal in the heart of the city – we noticed a sign in a window indicating a room for rent.

"J.J., there's a room in a private house. Let's check it out."

"What do you mean, Dee? We *have* a hotel room. What are we going to do with two?" I questioned, obviously confused.

"We haven't paid for it yet, and maybe that private room is cheaper and bigger. Let's look," Dee replied, not hearing a word as she charged ahead toward the canal house.

"Dee, this is *not* a good idea," I chided her.

Crazy ideas were not Dee's specialty; they were mine. And even this one, I thought, was too ridiculous for me.

"Come on, J.J. We're just going to look."

"But why *look* if we already have a room?" I asked, still confused.

Dee didn't answer as she was already up the stairs and knocking on the door, which was opened by a slender, young lady with two little children peering around her legs. Dee motioned for me to hurry, and, reluctantly, I followed.

The room was actually three times the size of our hotel room and half the price. A full-sized bed and two small tables with lamps spanned one side of the spacious room. A small dining table and two chairs sat near the door. That was all – there was space for a couch, chair, and dresser, but, obviously, funds were lacking and the bare essentials were supplied.

"We'll take it," I heard Dee say, unexpectedly.

"Are you *crazy*? What are you thinking?" I cried, pulling her aside.

"Well, we're going back to the hotel, and we'll try to sneak out without being seen. No official forms have been signed and no money paid."

"Dee, this is not a good idea," I said again – more firmly this time.

"Live on the wild side, J.J. It'll be fine. Come on. Let's go back to the hotel and get our luggage."

"That's the other point, Dee. Our luggage is already in our room. We lugged the bags all the way up three flights of stairs, and I'm pretty sure that I've gotten a hernia this time."

Dee seemed unconcerned.

I tried again. "If the bags were still in the lobby, there would be a greater possibility of my considering this idiotic plan."

As she plunged ahead submerged in thought, I knew that I was doomed. I may as well yield and get my luggage. As we entered, the hotel clerk was nowhere to be seen.

"See, what did I tell you? It will be a piece of cake," Dee smiled smugly as she scurried up the stairs.

I threw Dee a dubious look as I caught up with her. I was feeling very uncomfortable. Within five minutes, however, we were discreetly – no, deviously is a better word – descending the dark stairs, hoping that the lobby would still be empty. My luggage thumped down each stair as together the bags were too heavy to lift, and I didn't dare carry only one at a time in our desperate plan to escape. As we reached the bottom step, the hotel clerk suddenly appeared from the back room.

"Oh, oh, Dee. We're dead!" I whispered.

His spew of Italians words led us to believe that he wasn't happy. Pushing past us, he raced towards the door, bellowing "*polizia, polizia!*"

"Dee, he's yelling for the police! Now, what do we do?"

"Just hurry, J.J. We're leaving," Dee yelled with a determined demeanor that I had rarely seen in her before.

Dee whizzed past the screaming hotel clerk, and I was close behind, sloughing my bags. We bolted through the door and turned down a nearby, deserted alley, heading in the direction of the room we had most recently rented. From behind, we could still hear the distant voice yelling "*polizia.*" Walking as fast as possible, dragging our heavy luggage, our singular thought was escaping the slammer. The alley was narrow and dark, and we were hoping it would eventually lead to the main street. In addition, I was hoping that the alleyway didn't narrow at any point so that I'd be trapped – stuck – there with my overly-abundant, rotund bags.

Five minutes into the great escape, I stopped to catch my breath.

"That was a close call, Dee," I said, collapsing on top of my green bag. "You know, I can just hear my phone call home – 'Mom, I'm in an Italian prison. Tell my principal I'll be a few days late returning home. Ciao.'"

Laughingly, Dee tried to contribute to the conversation – "Mom, you'll be glad to know that I've been learning Italian. The most recent phrase I've learned is 'I need a lawyer!'"

By now, I had turned around several times to make sure that no *polizia* were pursuing us as we giggled at yet another precarious adventure.

After a five-minute rest, I suggested, "Let's see if this alley is going to lead to a main street or a dead end." Picking up our luggage, we slowly continued down the dark path to God-knows-where.

Eventually, we saw daylight plus people walking; we knew we were coming to a thoroughfare of some kind. Since no vehicles were allowed in Venice, it had to be a main pedestrian street. Emerging from the alley, we tried to get our bearings.

"There's the house with the room we rented," Dee said as she pointed down the street.

"Are you sure?" I questioned, no longer willing to trust Dee's judgment. After all, she had almost landed us in jail.

"Yes, I remember the house had green shutters trimmed in orange. Let's go," she answered, barging ahead.

"At least I don't see any *polizia*!" I added, still looking behind me with worried thoughts about seeing the inside of an Italian prison.

Graciously, the young mother welcomed us again although she spoke little English. However, we had become quite adept in sign language and pantomimes.

As we went to our room, we saw four eyes peering at us from behind a curtain.

"Those children are adorable," Dee commented. She waved to them, but they quickly disappeared, obviously too shy to make friends with strange people not speaking their language.

In the large, open room, there was plenty of space to put our luggage, unlike our "closet" in Holland or our "rafter room" in Paris. I took a moment to look at my travel stickers, to see how they had handled the escape. Many had torn and edges were turning up on some of my favorites. I remembered that I had brought glue – for what, I don't know – and decided that I'd repair my display of pictures later in the afternoon.

* * * * * * * * * * *

Venice was everything the books said it would be and more. What a spectacular city. Walking the maze of narrow, twisting streets and alleys proved to be an unending puzzle. We would just start to figure out where we were when suddenly we became confused and once again lost in the labyrinth of cobblestone alleyways and *calles.*

We focused on *Piazza San Marco* for one afternoon and evening. The gorgeous gardens, open markets, elegant cafes, and incredible street entertainers completely captivated us.

At one end of the square was the *Doges' Palace*, the official residence of the Venetian rulers. In the fourteenth century, the traditional Venetian architecture was broken with the construction of the palace in pink marble with delicate fretwork and spacious arches. The airy Gothic masterpiece was an outstanding, unbelievable structure in Venice.

At the other end of the Piazza was the spectacular *Basilica San Marco*. This cathedral blended architectural styles of the East and West, creating one of the greatest churches in Europe. The exterior of the Basilica owed its splendor to countless treasures from the Orient. Bronze horses, bas reliefs, column, and colored marbles brought from Constantinople in 1204 all enhanced the main façade. Included in the facing was a mosaic of the body of St. Mark being carried into the church.

The narthex of the thirteenth-century cathedral contained a spectacular Creation of the World, described in concentric circles and a floor patterned with mosaics in marble and colored glass. The interior of the church contained jewel-bedecked altars and the famous Ascension Dome, which featured a mosaic of Christ surrounded by angels, the twelve disciples, and the Virgin Mary. Covering not only the Dome but also the walls and floor of the church were 43,000 square feet of gleaming, golden mosaics, dating to the twelfth century. The Basilica was truly a masterpiece that captivated hundreds of visitors each day.

"What an incredible city, Dee. There's something really fascinating not only about *Piazza San Marco* but about Venice in general. Partially, I think it is the old, winding streets lined with the gaslights. Or maybe it's the hundreds of canals and gondolas. I feel as if I'm in a time warp, back in the 1200s. There's such romance yet mysterious ambiance in this wonderful, old Italian city. I wish we could stay longer."

"What do you mean? Why can't we stay?" Dee questioned.

"Well, I was looking at the calendar today. If we're going to get back for the start of school in mid-August, we better head for Rome soon, within the next few days," I answered.

"Gee, these weeks have flown by," Dee said, pondering how our trip could be coming to a close so soon. "When do you think we should leave?"

"I'm thinking that maybe we should go in a few days so we have plenty of time in Rome."

Dee was quiet as I looked at her. "What's wrong?"

"I wish I could visit the two towns where my grandparents lived," she answered.

"Why can't we, Dee? That's a wonderful idea. We'll just not spend as much time in Rome. Seeing those cities would be so exciting for you."

"They're out of the way, J.J., and I'm not sure the train goes there."

"Well, let's rent a car," I answered spontaneously. Of course, spontaneity was one of my less-than-desirable traits, and I certainly hadn't considered this wild plan very carefully.

"Gosh, I don't know. Do you think it's safe to drive over here? The Europeans are maniacs behind the wheel of a car, you know," Dee noted with hesitation in her voice. "You've seen them drive in Paris and Amsterdam, and the Italians are especially nuts."

"I think that once we're out of the city, the rural areas should be safer. The cities are dangerous just because of all of the congestion – too many cars with too few wide boulevards." I paused. "Well, what do you think?" Silently, I was beginning to wonder if I was insane to suggest this, but I was in too deep now to back out.

"If you think it's okay, then I'm game," Dee was beaming at the prospect of visiting her grandparents' birthplace.

We lingered in Venice another day. On the last evening as we entered the house to go to our room, we again glimpsed the four big eyes from behind the curtain. I had bought some candy and two puzzles, and Dee had purchased some little dolls at the market that morning with the intent of giving them to the two small children, whose eyes were the only things with which we were truly acquainted.

One by one we held up the presents, pulling first the candy and then the puzzles and dolls from our bags. Four tiny hands pulled the curtain aside, revealing two precious little dark-haired girls dressed in faded, thin dresses. We motioned for them to come as we knelt to their height.

Cautiously, the children – their eyes shining and faces beaming – crept toward us. We were sure they didn't get many presents or toys as the mother's budget seemed slim, and we had never observed a father although he was probably present at intervals. The four frail hands grasped at the presents dubiously, curling their tiny fingers around the gifts, as we nodded our heads "yes" all the while. They took them, darting from the room with their treasures. We grinned to each other, wondering how late they would lay under their covers playing with their newly acquired gifts.

Early the next morning, we left Venice in search of Rome. Our plans were to see Rome's sights first before renting the car. It would give us a few more days to muster enough courage to get behind the wheel of an Italian car, which could go as fast as 250-300 kilometers per hour. That thought alone sent me into a tailspin. I definitely was wondering what kind of mess I had gotten us into now.

Truly, I'm a moron, I thought, as I looked out the train window to see the Italian sports cars propelling themselves in and out of lanes at speeds that I couldn't even fathom. Like bats shot out of hell, they bulleted the highway, daring anyone to stop them.

Good grief, I'm going to be behind the wheel of one of those cars.

Chapter 19

The Wrong Hairdryer...The Wrong Room

Arriving in Rome, we got a hotel near the famous and crowded Spanish Steps. Even though it was an exclusive part of Rome, we found a reasonably priced hotel. Thousands of tourists bustled both day and night around the Spanish Steps, built in 1720. Below the Steps sprawled the square, *Piazza di Spagna,* with the spectacular French church, *Trinita*, looming at the top. The fantastic staircase ascended in three ramps from the piazza, interrupted by terraces, displaying an immense array of vivid, pink azaleas. The *Piazza di Spagna* – the most famous square in Rome – had long been the haunt of foreign visitors, musicians, and artists selling their wares. Still today, it is one of the most incredible sights in the city.

Immediately, we decided that Rome was going to be another *ultimate* city for us. It was an absolutely awesome metropolis with wealth, ancient history, culture, art, music, fashion, aristocracy, cuisine, and religion. It had everything imaginable, and we were once again in love.

We ended our second day near the *Pantheon*, the Roman temple completed in AD 125. The oculus – a hole at the top of the dome – provided the only light in the structure. Because the oculus – thirty feet across – opened to the sky, the heavens seemed to descend into the temple as the congregation's prayers rose freely to God. The church was a masterpiece of perfect proportion as well as one of the most important and also best-preserved temples in Rome.

We sat adjacent to the *Pantheon*, eating gelato – the Italian version of American ice cream but much tastier and less fattening – and thinking back over our first extraordinary day in ancient Rome.

"In these two days, what has been your favorite, J.J.?" Dee questioned, scooping strawberry gelato into her mouth. "I have no idea. We have seen so much," I said, stopping to think. "Yesterday, seeing the Forum and standing on the site where Julius Caesar was cremated and Mark Anthony delivered his famous speech was absolutely incredible for me. Teaching *Julius Caesar* will never be the same again," I smiled, thinking of the Forum where not only business transactions were performed in ancient Rome but also all public life of the citizens revolved. It was there that the assemblies of the Senate, elections of the Magistrates, and religious ceremonies occurred.

"But I really *loved* the *Colosseum*, too," I continued. "It was really bigger than I thought it would be. Imagine watching the deadly gladiatorial combats and wild animal fights staged in that arena." Dee nodded as she bit into the long, circular cookie that had been stuck into the middle of the gelato.

The immense amphitheatre, which the Romans called the *Colosseum*, was started in 72 AD by Vespasian, who used Jewish prisoners as workers. The gladiators, who were trained to fight until death, cultivated the war-like spirit that had made the Romans into world conquerors. Of course, the wild beasts increased the horror of the spectacles seen in the *Colosseum*. Being 615 feet in length and 158 feet high, the arena was built to accommodate 80,000 spectators. The monumental size and practical organization for producing spectacles and controlling crowds made it one of ancient Rome's greatest architectural monuments.

I paused to further ponder our two days. "And then there was the *Piazza Navona*."

Already Dee was chuckling.

"Okay, I know why you're laughing, but I didn't know that the couple had just gotten married," I remarked.

"Your first clue should have been the girl in the white dress," Dee snickered.

We had been standing in front of a small church near the *Piazza,* and I asked the well-dressed man next to me if he would snap our picture. Before he could answer, the flash of a camera captured the man – who happened to be the groom – with his bride.

"Well, her dress didn't look like a wedding dress to me," I responded. "But, yes, I felt like a complete fool."

"He probably didn't even understand English, J.J., because he didn't answer," Dee tried to console me.

"He didn't respond because the pigeon flew over, splattering the cameraman. The groom was in shock."

Dee let out a howl, and we both laughed as we thought of the unfortunate man who had been in the wrong place at the wrong time.

"Well, anyway, I really liked the *Piazza Navona.* You could see why it had been the lavish social center of the city centuries ago because so much is still happening there. The open market had some of the best oil paintings that I've seen in all of Europe. I sort of wish that I had bought that small one of the *Colosseum.*"

Even though the painting has been small, my problem was where to put it to get home. I really couldn't find another corner in my carry-on to put even a toothpick, and I knew it was time to discard more clothes and half-emptied bottles. If I could have rolled it, it could have gone into my poster tube. But this painting was already framed and so with regret, I didn't buy it.

"Oh, and that fountain in the center...what was it called?" I asked.

"Oh, I think it was the Fountain of Rivers, wasn't it?" Dee replied.

"Yeah, the Fountain of Rivers. It was really extraordinary – rather flamboyant – don't you think?"

"Yeah, it was. I loved that fountain," Dee interjected as she wiped gelato from her mouth with a napkin, "but the *Trevi Fountain* was my favorite. I've always wanted to see it ever since I saw *Three Coins in a Fountain* years ago. It's actually smaller than I imagined. Oh, by the way, I threw my coins in so that means that I'll be back to Rome someday," she smiled broadly.

I, too, had loved that fountain which seemed to appear from nowhere at the end of several narrow alleyways. Built in 1735, the statues in the fountain depicted a maiden showing soldiers a beautiful source of pure water and Agrippa, a Roman statesman, explaining an aqueduct plan to emperor Caesar Augustus. A statue of Neptune – god of the seas – on a shell-shaped chariot pulled by winged horses occupied the center of the fountain.

"And today I saw my other favorite – St. Peter's Basilica," Dee continued, pulling me from my reverie. "Michelangelo's *Pieta* was fabulous. I can't believe he was only 25 when he created that remarkable sculpture. You could almost feel the pain of Mary as she held Christ on her lap. And then there were those huge, marble columns throughout the cathedral. 'Wow' is all I can say about that church."

Before I saw the Basilica, I had no conceivable vision of the spectrum of the St. Peter's. Even as I stood looking at it, I couldn't grasp the sprawling drama of it. A series of 284 columns arranged in four rows created an elliptical shape in the vast courtyard of the church. Five entrances flanked by gigantic marble columns led into the narthex of the cathedral. Above the central doorway was the fabulous mosaic of Giotto depicting an allegorical ship carrying the disciples.

A sculptured bronze door led directly into the Basilica, and we realized we had entered the largest, most grandiose cathedral in the world. Vast in scale and awe-inspiring in its effect, the Catholic Church had celebrated their belief in God through a splendid fusion of Renaissance and Baroque art.

I was savoring the last of my vanilla gelato served with fruit as Dee continued. "Well, how can I forget the Sistine

Chapel at the Vatican. I've never seen such a display of frescos. They were...well, overwhelming...awe-inspiring."

Michelangelo frescoed the ceiling in the Sistine Chapel between 1508 and 1512. The Creation of the World and The Fall of Man revealed colors of unexpected vibrancy – brilliant oranges, greens, reds, and yellows. The Original Sin depicted Adam and Eve tasting the forbidden fruit with Satan represented as a snake with a woman's body.

"How can we even get a taste of Rome in only a couple of days? What an incredible ancient city." Dee was just babbling now, and I let her. I enjoyed silently reminiscing about the two wonderful days we had experienced in Rome.

Finally, I asked, "Would you rather see more of Rome or rent a car and go to the villages?" I was halfway hoping that this was my chance of getting out of this idea that only a lunatic could have considered in the first place.

"That's a tough call," Dee answered, pondering the question for a full minute before replying. "I guess I'd really like to get the car and find the villages of my grandparents. I'd kick myself after getting home if I didn't."

With my hopes daunted, I was kicking myself right then that I had ever suggested the plan. However, I tried to think optimistically. "Well, okay, day after tomorrow we'll rent an automobile, leave the big city for a few days, and see the Italian countryside."

Silently, I hoped that the driving wouldn't be as horrendous as I thought, and Dee's broad smile helped me to believe that we had made the right decision – these would be lifetime memories about her family that would be unsurpassed.

* * * * * * * * *

The next day, we retraced some of our steps in Rome, reviewing some of the spectacular sights that warranted a second visit – St. Peter's Basilica and the Forum.

We revisited our favorite local restaurant, *Porto di Ripetta*, near our hotel. It served the best *Saltimbocca alla Romana* in all of Rome. The tasty dish – made with ham, veal, and sage – became something we both began to crave every evening. Coupled with the soup of the day and spinach-filled *tortelloni*, we also took a glass of Frascati wine. We had discovered this locally bottled white wine, and Dee now tried to fathom how to get some home in her already over-stuffed luggage. Of course, we concluded a dish of gelato with every meal.

It was before our gelato on that last evening in Rome that we met Martha, a Latin teacher from New Jersey. She had just completed a tour with high school students. They had returned home, and she remained behind for an extended stay. Her knowledge of Rome was remarkable. Martha talked about Rome's vast niches and crannies of which we had never even heard. She talked about the *Bocca della Verita* (The Mouth of Truth), and because it especially intrigued both Dee and me, she offered to escort us there. The *Bocco della Verita* was erected in the portico of the Church of Santa Maria in Cosmedia, which was already closed when we arrived at 9 o'clock. But because the portico was outside the church, we were able to see the incredible Mouth of Truth.

It was a huge circular stone mask from the twelfth century, which contained eyes, nose, and an open mouth. Its name was derived from an ancient legend: if a witness – whose truthfulness was in doubt – placed his hand into the open mouth, the mask would bite him if he were guilty or lying. A stone mask biting someone is inconceivable but then it *is* a legend. According to Martha, The *Boco della Verita* sees hundreds of visitors each day, and we were glad that we had seen him. It wouldn't have been possible if it hadn't been for our friend, Martha, who took time to escort us to the church.

* * * * * * * * * *

The next morning was our last in Rome, and I arose before Dee, had showered, and was drying my hair when she got up.

"Today's the day we leave," Dee blurted out as she stretched in an attempt to wake up.

Only half listening, I had my own problems. "Dee, something is wrong with the hairdryer," I said, flipping the switch a couple of times in an attempt to turn it on.

"It was fine yesterday, wasn't it?" Dee inquired, throwing off the covers and sitting up.

"Yeah, it was," I answered.

"Here, let me see," she said, taking the dryer and flipping the switch. "Umm, don't know."

"I noticed the hotel clerk in Paris loaning one to a guest," I said, still jiggling the switch in a final attempt to get it to work. "Maybe this hotel has an extra one that they loan to people."

"It's worth a try. Why don't you ask? I'll need to use it, too."

I trotted down the stairs to the lobby, wet hair and all. There, behind the reception desk stood the most gorgeous man alive. He was a little short, but his dark hair, olive skin, and unbelievably fluid, brown eyes made up for his height. I struggled to read his name – Angelo.

"Sir," I said, eyeing him up and down, "are there any hairdryers available?" I was suddenly conscious of my tacky, wet hair and attempted to unsuccessfully flick it out of my eyes. "My hairdryer died this morning."

"It died?" the "hunk" asked with a blank look covering his face.

"Well, it quit working," I answered with a silly smile.

"Oh, I see. Well, I don't have one here at the desk, but there's a hairdryer in a room upstairs."

Angelo's English was perfect – only a slight accent,

which added to his charm. Everything about him was perfect – except for his age, maybe. I guessed him to be about 45, a little too old for me. It didn't matter, though. Angelo was totally exquisite whatever his age. My eyes never left his body as I tried to imagine what he must have looked like at 25. I was drooling now and made a feeble attempt to pull my thoughts back to the present conversation.

"Well, may I borrow it?" I stammered.

"It's a built-in dryer, miss." Angelo grinned at me as he continued to flip through the hotel receipts. Italian men seem to have a way of looking down but still eyeing – well, flirting with – the person with whom they are talking. I don't know how they do it.

"Oh, I see." My hopes were fading – not only to use the hairdryer but also to continue the conversation with Angelo.

"But the people in that room have checked out already, so you may use the dryer. You'll just have to go to their room. If you don't mind doing that, then it's no problem."

"That would be fine." By now, I was struggling to remember what we were even talking about as I stretched my neck to check out his ring finger. No ring.

"I'll show you the room if you'll follow me."

Angelo flashed me a movie-star smile as I tried to think what to say to *that* statement. I wanted to say, "Angelo, I'll follow you anywhere…."

Finally, I was able to sputter, "Okay, thank you."

As we went up the staircase, I tried to chat intelligently with Angelo, who by now I had decided must be a Roman god. No human being could possess a body as well as a face that incredibly gorgeous. And not married? That meant that no woman wanted him? Quickly I reprimanded myself for the stupid thought. You dope, *every* woman must want him.

"Your English is very good, Angelo." I tried not to fumble the words, yet the sentence seemed trite.

212

"Well, thank you. I lived in Florida for two years," he added, his eyes melting into mine as I dreamed of *so many* possibilities with Angelo.

"Really? No wonder you speak English so well. You hardly have an accent." That, too, sounded lame, I thought. Every American must tell him that. "Where did you live in Florida?" I said, trying desperately to keep the conversation rolling.

"In Miami. I went to the university there, studying oceanography."

My mind was racing – like when too many facts are fed to you at once and you can't register them quickly enough. I was trying to visualize Angelo in his swim trunks, dozens of bikini-clad girls surrounding him on the beach. He was tanned and had a beach towel hanging round his neck. A change of scenery took Angelo to the university campus as he strolled to class under the direction of two blondes, clutching tightly to his arms. His khaki pants and polo shirt completed his collegiate look as he smiled and blew kisses to his entourage of girls.

My reverie was interrupted with Angelo's voice. "Well, here's the room, miss."

I wondered how long I had been daydreaming because we were now rounding a corner, standing in front of a door.

"Oh, okay," I said, attempting to return to reality. "I need to get my friend. She wants to use the hairdryer, also."

"That's fine. I'll unlock the door and leave it open a little," he said, retrieving a master key from his coat pocket.

"Okay. Thank you so much. It was very nice talking with you."

Angelo nodded, smiled, and bowed slightly. "My pleasure, miss."

Wow, I thought – Wow! Why can't American men be chivalrous like that?

Returning to my room still in a daze, I found Dee out of the shower, hair dripping.

"Got a dryer, but we need to go to another room. It's installed in the bathroom, and the people have already checked out." I decided to tell Dee about the hairdryer, keeping Angelo as my secret for a moment longer.

"Okay, let's go," Dee said, grabbing a towel to dry her hair.

As we climbed the stairs, I couldn't contain myself any longer. Knowing my parents would never approve of an older man, I thought I'd give Dee a chance at the love-of-my-life.

"Dee, I found an Italian guy who is perfect for you. He's perfect for me, too, but he's a little too old."

"Wait a minute. If he's too old for you, then he's also too old for me. I'm two years younger than you are, remember?"

"Yes, but he's a full-blooded Italian, and your father would love him regardless of his age," I continued. I was thinking that if she took Angelo home, I could at least look at him often.

"Exactly, how old is this man, and, by the way, where did you find him?"

"Well, he's probably 45 or so, and he's the gorgeous hotel clerk downstairs," I blurted out. "Dee, he's a true 'hunk' if I've ever seen one."

"J.J., don't be crazy. My father wouldn't let me date a man of 45 – Italian or not. He's probably married anyhow."

"No, there's no ring, Dee," I quickly chimed in.

"Doesn't mean a thing with Italian men, J.J. Hey, where is this room anyway?" I had a feeling that Dee was trying to change the conversation before it got too deep.

"Well, this is pretty stupid, but I didn't look at the room number. I'm afraid that I was focused on Angelo. But it's on the fourth floor, I *think*."

"Angelo? So you're on a first name basis?" she questioned.

"It was on his nametag, Dee."

She nodded, returning to the hairdryer situation. "Oh, well, then what do you mean you *think* this room is on the fourth floor?"

"Don't freak out, Dee. Angelo left the door open for us. Here's the fourth floor. Let's look around this corner."

Peeking around the corner, I spied the room.

"See there's the door cracked open."

Even in the dark, we could see the bathroom as we walked in. We didn't bother to turn on the bedroom light but rather just flipped on the bathroom light and retrieved the hairdryer from the wall. Dee turned it on and started to dry her hair.

"Since it's a European dryer, I guess I don't have to keep it on low heat. Only my American hairdryer will blow a fuse on high," Dee added with a giggle.

I didn't hear anymore of her conversation because out of the corner of my eye, I spied something – something that moved. Turning to obtain a full view of the moving object, I stood with my mouth gaping.

Quickly, I tugged on Dee's sleeve. She was still chattering about the dryer but turned, stopping mid-sentence.

"Good grief, J.J. Who the heck is that? You said the room was vacant!" she exclaimed.

Sitting straight up in bed was a Japanese man. Unbelievably, a pink and white shower cap covered his hair.

"This is...unreal," I stammered. "Let's get out of here."

Suddenly, the little guy began talking a mile a minute – not in English, of course, in Japanese. As he waved his arms in a frantic motion, his voice grew louder and higher in pitch until he was screaming a gibberish of words at us.

Dee and I dropped the dryer and shot from the room. As we bulleted past the man, he bellowed at us, spewing his innermost thoughts concerning our uninvited intrusion.

I tried to express my apologies with a few quick bows

and "sorry, sorry," but he continued his nonstop chiding in a loud falsetto voice. Amazingly, his wife was lying next to him, still asleep.

As we reached the hall and slammed the door, I turned to Dee. "Perhaps I got the wrong room," I said dryly with a straight face.

Dee stifled her laughter until we rounded the corner and were out of earshot. Bursting into uncontrollable cackling, we both sank onto the floor, nearly rolling down the stairs. Meanwhile, I was trying to unravel the puzzle and comprehend exactly what had gone wrong.

"Obviously, I made a *big* mistake."

"No! What makes you think that?" Dee replied sarcastically, her eyes twinkling as she wiped the tears running down her face.

Trying to mentally sort through the fiasco, I realized that several things could have gone wrong. "Well, obviously, I got the wrong room, but maybe I chose the wrong floor, too."

"Gosh, J.J., why didn't you check the room number?"

"Sorry, sorry," I answered, bowing and using my newly acquired Japanese technique. "You know, the really strange coincidence is that the man's door was cracked open. Why in the world would his door be open when he was in bed?" I asked more to myself than to Dee.

"More importantly, what was the purpose of the shower cap?" Dee asked as we again broke into uncontrollable giggles.

"Well, let's go up one more flight of stairs and see if there's a room with the door open," I suggested after our fit of laughter subsided.

"I don't know if I want to follow you. I really don't trust your judgment right now," Dee said, deliberation sounding in her voice.

"Come on. I remember having misgivings about your judgment in Venice, but I went along with changing hotels

– even at the expense of possibly landing in the clinker," I grinned.

As we rounded the corner on the next floor, there was a room with the door slightly ajar.

"There it is," I said, proud of my discovery.

"I refuse to walk in there," Dee said. *"You first."*

I peered through the door. As my eyes adjusted to the dark, there was an unmade bed – sheets and comforter pulled down – with no one in it.

"This is the place," I said, confidently.

"Not to be repetitious, but *you first.*"

"Okay, okay," I said, fumbling to find the light switch and then walking into the bathroom. "The room is empty, Dee. Come on."

"You know, J.J., I'm never going to trust you again," Dee laughed. "That was hilarious, but I wonder what that man thought of us!"

"Actually, I'm not too worried about what *he* thought of *us*. After all, he was a bit eccentric himself – a shower cap on his head and his door open."

The incident proved to be only the beginning of a very eventful day. We had had some crazy adventures on the train, but we were about to enter into a new world of escapades – life in a small European car on the suicidal highways of Italy.

Chapter 20

A Suicidal Mission

Renting a car was no problem. Saying goodbye to Angelo was. My heart was breaking as we checked out and handed him our room key. He flashed us a smile and a wink as he took a moment from the other arriving travelers to wish us well.

"I think that he knows that you're in love with him, J.J.," Dee whispered as we toted our now-elephantine bags from the lobby.

"I'm not in love with him. It's just that he was a once-in-a-lifetime man, Dee," I retorted, exiting the hotel as I took one final glance at him over my shoulder.

"He was gorgeous, J.J., but I assure you that *his* place is here at the hotel and *ours* is on the road to Todi and Assisi," she grinned, also taking one last look at the man of our dreams as we closed the hotel door.

Dee and I walked to the Avis car rental office a block from our hotel. I was literally dragging my bags. People eyeing them could now decipher my European route through the glossy pictures plastered all over the sides. With no space left on the green one, stickers of the Eiffel Tower, Arc de Triomphe, and I Love Paris spilled over unto my brown luggage. The clove of garlic tied to the carry-on's handle had been discarded the day before. It had grown quite fragrant in the heat, and it found its way into a garbage can next to our hotel. Tugging the bags – cowbell clanging against my St. Bernard key chain that hung on my carry-on – was a real effort as we made our way down the narrow, winding street, directly behind the Spanish Steps. The block seemed more like two or three as we struggled to get to the car rental office.

As we entered the Avis office, the agent behind the desk sported the usual dark, handsome look of a pure Italian, topped with an award-winning smile. Dressed in an Avis red sports jacket, he politely asked for identification, and we pulled out our American drivers' licenses, passports, and a credit card. He gave us a contract to fill out, including the opportunity to buy extra insurance, costing an additional 10,000 lira a day. Dee started to shake her head, just as I interrupted with "yes, we'll take it." Dee flashed me a questioning look.

"Dee, I'm not taking any chances. I want extra coverage on that car. These Europeans can be a little wild. Even *you* said that the Italians are maniacs" I whispered to Dee.

She nodded. "Yeah, you're right."

"I assume that they won't be quite as crazy on the highway as in the city, but I just want to be on the safe side," I concluded.

We signed the contract for a week's rental, got a map, and received directions onto the major highway outside of Rome, which headed north through Italy.

"When you get out of the garage, turn right. At the second stop light, turn right again on *Via Nationale*. Go three streets, and if you look left, you'll see the highway," the Avis agent concluded.

"Thank you, sir," I said.

That sounds simple, I thought, but I won't make any bets that it truly is that easy. I had heard European directions before, and they never were as easy as they sounded. Sometimes the Europeans counted an alley as a street and sometimes they didn't. If they said to go four streets, it was always tenuous that you would be able to find that fourth street on the first try. I had also heard, "Oh, that place is only a couple of blocks...a ten-minute walk," In reality it would be two miles, taking an hour. Trying to figure out European directions and their estimated times were always arduous tasks for us Americans.

As we exited the building into the car lot, Dee suggested, "J.J., why don't you drive first? I'll navigate."

"Okay," I quickly agreed. I didn't relish the thought of driving in Rome, but I figured that I could easily handle the highway driving. And according to our directions, we only had a few blocks before we were out of Rome proper.

Looking through the rows of dozens of compact European cars, we finally located Row 12, car number 45, and found that a shiny, new red Opal had been assigned to us. Black cloth interior, stick shift, radio, but no air-conditioning. We had assumed this since Europe wasn't really introduced to that luxury yet. Having only one key assigned bothered me until I realized that we had to use the key to lock the car. No worry about locking the key inside – my only hope was that we didn't lose it.

The trunks were tiny, but we tried to maneuver our four bulging bags into the small cubicle of space. The two larger ones were stuffed into the trunk, and the two carry-ons were squeezed into the backseat.

Dee's luggage had become considerably more bulky since we arrived in Rome. The various souvenirs that she had picked up in Paris for her siblings – T-shirts, perfume, berets, and small wooden toys – had been packed easily. The only souvenirs that were cumbersome were the two swords bought in Spain. I had tried to dissuade her from purchasing them, but she wanted a memory from Madrid other than the bullfight, and the swords seemed to "fit the bill." She had trouble deciding where to put them, and, eventually, she stuffed the handles into the side pocket of her carry-on as the rest of the sword stuck out at a threatening angle. Today, they would be deemed weapons, and we would be considered terrorists, but in the '70s, no one gave that a second thought. However, Dee's luggage was now receiving as many glances from passersby as mine was.

However, souvenirs from Rome presented a problem all their own to Dee with leather products readily available at the open markets. Bargaining was the game, and she purchased leather purses for three sisters – a great buy at 5,000 lira (five dollars) a piece. A leather coat and two pairs of Italian shoes found their way into her larger suitcase. They were the real challenge, stuffed and crammed into the remaining space, which was daily growing smaller.

Settling ourselves into the car, I didn't know it at the time, but I would now be faced with a major challenge. I had always driven a stick shift at home, but this car was different. The diagram next to the shift showed me how to get to each gear, but reverse seemed impossible.

"Maybe the motor has to be running in order to get the car into reverse," Dee suggested.

I started the motor but still no luck.

"Perhaps I'm just not getting the angle right," I said, trying still again to get it into the reverse gear.

Nope.

Sitting for perhaps ten minutes playing with the gearshift, I was about to give up in despair when Dee had an idea. She pulled up on the stick shift and then pulled back. The car slipped into reverse!

And then there was the emergency brake, which had to be used with a manual automobile. First of all, we couldn't even find it. Normally next to the gearshift, it wasn't there. No, not down by the pedals – we looked everywhere. At last I looked to my left I found it slightly tucked under the seat.

"This is stupid," I said. "Why can't they make these cars like the American autos?" I asked in frustration. "Or at least so an American can figure them out."

With a sigh of relief and a whimpish smile, I backed out of the rental garage and onto a side street. My directions were to turn right. It was narrow and dark – as all inner-city European streets seem to be – with old buildings on both sides and cars parked every which way, even on the sidewalks. It was one-way traffic, and when I got to the second stoplight, it, too, was one-way, going the wrong direction. We went to the next street and turned right. After two blocks, it ended in a dead end.

By now, we were confused and a bit exasperated. We drove back, trying other possibilities, never finding *Via Nationale*. We tried to read the map and look at what street we were on, but it was useless.

"I had a feeling it wasn't going to be as simple as he said," I concluded.

We floundered our way from one alleyway to another – the Italians actually called them streets – horns honking on all sides, people yelling a myriad of Italian phrases from car windows. At one point, I actually drove up onto a sidewalk, thinking it was a narrow street. That was an embarrassing moment, but no worse than any of the other crazy incidents on the trip.

And then, nearly hitting a dog when I turned a corner, I swerved, only to barely miss a motorbike coming directly towards us. With sweaty palms tightly clutched to the wheel, I drove for thirty-five minutes in complete frenzy. Obviously driving in Rome took talent that I didn't possess. Was it talent or insanity that these Italians had, I wondered? At that moment, I was too crazed – and hysterical – to sort through the chaotic situation.

Accidentally – or else God decided to spare us – we found a large, green sign at an intersection, pointing to Highway H8. We took a right, and within minutes we were headed onto the freeway. I breathed a sigh of relief as my little red Opal pulled out of the tiny, crowded Roman streets onto a four-lane highway. The relief lasted a total of fifteen seconds, however, as suddenly I felt as if I was in the midst of the Indianapolis 500 as first a Fiat, then two Mercedes, and finally a yellow Ferrari zipped and zoomed on all sides of us. With our windows wide open for air, the noise was deafening, giving us the feeling that we were sitting directly on a racetrack.

Wide-eyed and completely unnerved, I screeched to Dee above the roar of passing cars, "Is this the highway or a race track? What's the speed limit?" White-knuckled and bent over the steering wheel, I was totally overwhelmed by the amazing speeds. Attempting to see the cars in front, in back, and all sides, I knew I didn't dare take my eyes off the road long enough to search for a speed limit sign. Cars were racing upon us like vultures after a dead animal.

Dee had turned a pale shade of white and had clutched the door handle with a death grip.

"I don't think there is a speed limit, and these Italians are maniacs. Surely, this isn't their normal way of driving!" she exclaimed.

I didn't answer because I was frantically trying to maneuver my little red car into the right-hand lane, used by the elderly – and hopefully – the sane and sober drivers.

Attempting to gain a grip on the current predicament, I glanced at my speedometer. "I'm going 100 kilometers per hour, and we're the slowest car on the road. Sunday sightseers are going faster than we are. Will you look at that – a little one-cylinder motor scooter just passed us."

Dee was laughing despite her fear, which was still evident on her face.

"Our speedometer says that our little car will go 240 kilometers an hour," I screeched again, above the roar of two Fiats. "If I'm doing 100, then those cars passing us must be doing 180 or more. This is unbelievable. There must be an easier and safer way for these Italians to commit suicide – and murder," I exclaimed, trying to claim the slow lane as mine and remain calm on the road with every deranged person in the world passing me.

"How fast is 100? Do you know?" Dee questioned.

"I have no idea," I replied.

That evening we converted kilometers into miles with the help of the guidebook – 100 kph was 65 mph and 180 kph was 110 mph. Our red Opal could do a whopping 145 mph or 240 kph.

Slowly – within the next fifteen minutes – I started to gain a little confidence as I became accustomed to the frantic pace of the Italian drivers. However, trying to talk Dee into driving was fruitless.

"No way. It was your crazy idea to rent a car. You drive" was all she could say.

Within the next half hour I picked my speed up to 130 – so that I wasn't a hazard on the road for driving too *slowly* – but I still wasn't able to pass one single car. A little black jaguar was upon us and passed us before I even saw it in the mirror. I only heard "zzzzzip" as I saw a streak of black and decided it had to be going 300 or more. Seeing the car twenty minutes later only confirmed the fact that the high speeds were suicidal. Wrapped around a fatal post on the median were the remains of the car. The police and an ambulance were already on the scene. The sight of the totally mangled car – turned upside down and literally bent around the post – led us to believe that there was no hope for any passengers.

After an hour of psychotic madness on the road, I had a suggestion. "Dee, you're the navigator. Look at the map and see if we can get off 'hell's highway.' Maybe there's a back road we can take that might be less suicidal. What are the names of the villages of your grandparents?"

"My grandmother was from Todi, and my grandfather lived in Assisi. The towns are close together. I'll look at the map. Getting off this highway would be a great idea," Dee answered, attempting to read the map, with one hand still clutching the door handle.

I must have been delirious, but at this point in time, foolishly, I still trusted Dee's ability to read the map.

"There's a road within the next few miles that should lead us toward Todi. It's Route A45."

"You watch for it, Dee. I'm too busy watching these crazed idiots." At least ten "zzzzips," "zzzzaps," and "zzzzooms" occurred every few minutes.

Before long we saw a red sign for Route A45, and I proceeded to look for the exit. Slowing down to 90 kilometers, we soon saw the road, eased our way onto the exit, and headed north, leaving the Indianapolis 500 to the Italians.

As my nerves relaxed and I gained feeling in my fingers after my death grip on the wheel, I realized that no cars were zapping past us, and I could stay at 90 and not be a road hazard. I started to soak up the beauty of the lush, Italian landscape. Purple mountains had begun to appear in the distance – majestic and snowcapped. The small green hills in the foreground had circular rows of vineyards, crawling up the sides – all staked and perfectly spaced. A green plush carpet of grass was laid in all directions, and I was entranced by the beauty of the Italian countryside.

However, somewhere between the exit from the highway and the mountains, the Italians had forgotten to mark the back roads. Either that or else we were not intelligent enough to figure out how to read or find them. We drove for twenty minutes, making twists and turns, and somehow, we seemed to be going in a circle, passing the same landmarks several times.

"Dee, this is the second time we've gone over this bridge, and we saw that farmhouse earlier."

"Yeah, I know. I just don't know what we're doing wrong," Dee commented, looking at the map again.

"I see Route B24 to the right. Where does it go?"

"I don't know. It's not on the map," Dee commented. "But why don't you take it? At least we'll be heading toward the mountains which is the direction we want to go."

Before long, I was sure that our newly found route was a mistake. Well, more than a mistake – a total disaster.

"Dee, this road is beginning to look like a cow path. No wonder it isn't on the map. I think, it was an old Roman road used by Caesar. I saw a sign leading back to the suicidal highway that we were on originally. I think that highway is our only hope until we can find Route A45 again." Goats, sheep, and cows slowly sauntered across the road on their way to pasture. I felt an impending calamity if I stayed on the road. I was sure that we'd end up in the middle of a mud-covered pond or, worse yet, a huge mound of manure.

"Okay, whatever you say," Dee commented, her eyes still glued to the map, trying to read the small print as we sped over the dirt and gravel that now contained foot-deep bumps and ruts. We bounced along, and I prayed that we didn't get a flat tire as the clouds of dust encircled our car. Finally, we were forced to close the windows until we found a paved surface. Our shiny, red Opal had taken on an overall rugged look, with mud now splattered on the sides from our trek on the ancient Roman road leading to nowhere.

However, in the process of returning to the Highway H8, we ran upon Route A45.

"That was luck," Dee said proudly as if she had led us directly to the lost route herself. I nodded, knowing that I had lost all confidence in Dee's map-reading abilities.

Uneventfully, we continued on A45 for the next fifteen minutes, and as the mountain drew nearer, we could see cars winding up the side.

"Look at the cars up there. How did they ever reach that road twisting around the mountain?" Dee asked.

"I don't know, and I don't want to find out because mountain driving scares me. Hey, Route A45 stays on flat land, doesn't it?" Suddenly, I was worried.

"Yes, according to the map, it bypasses the mountains, J.J. Don't worry," Dee smiled. She actually seemed confident with that statement. More than anything, I wanted to believe her. However, I kept my eye on the road twisting around the side of the mountain. Fearfully, I wondered if it wasn't a main road because of the number of cars traveling on it. Silently, I prayed.

Before long, the realization that there was no road that

227

bypassed the mountains was evident. Just as the old adage went, "All roads lead to Rome," the adage of that day was, "All roads lead into the mountains."

"Dee, we're going straight into the mountains. We'll soon learn how those cars reached that winding mountain road because we're going to be on it." I wanted to cry.

Driving a mountain road in the United Stated is one thing – driving a mountain road in Italy is an entirely different dilemma. Dangerously narrow with only two lanes that twist back and forth, no side guardrails, roads only partially paved, and unbelievable corkscrew turns would accurately describe the mountain road that we encountered.

Aside from the bad road, people seemed to forget they were driving in extremely dangerous circumstances. Their speed assumed that of flat ground – at least the speed I drove on flat ground – as they zipped past me doing 140.

"Dee, would you like to drive?" I asked as we reached a nose-bleed height with no rails on the side of the road to keep us from plunging thousands of feet into the gorge.

"No, J.J. Reading the map and keeping us on track takes a great deal of talent and concentration, and I'm finally getting the hang of it. Thanks, anyway," she answered, dead serious.

I glanced at her and wondered if she was being sarcastic or if she believed what she was saying. Did she really think that it took talent, or worse yet, did she really believe that she was "getting the hang of it"? I made no further comment as I saw a giant hairpin curve looming ahead of me.

I knew I didn't dare glance off the mountain trail for long, but from time to time, I flashed a look to my right to see the beautiful view down the side of the mountain. Green valleys, crystal blue lakes, and clear mountain steams could be seen in clearings that were void of the tall mountain birch. I wanted to stop and feast my eyes, but there were no pull offs.

Again my mind wandered to the flat-tire situation.

What would a person with a flat do? If we got one, where would we pull off? There was no shoulder. With that thought in mind, I worried that around any bend or cork-screw, I might encounter someone in my lane with his car jacked up. How would I stop in time? Sweat poured down my face as I kept my fears to myself since Dee seemed to have all she could handle as navigator. Her eyes seemed first glued to the map and then to the road, all the while her hand still clenching the door handle.

I finally spotted a sign for what I thought to be a rest stop. Exhausted, I made a suggestion. "Hey, Dee, I just saw a sign for a place to stop. I need a break."

"Great. I could use a rest, too. Being the navigator is a strenuous job. I'm totally bushed."

I looked at her out of the corner of my eye. Knowing that she was clueless as to what I had been up against, I decided to say nothing. Besides, it was obvious that she was trying to pull herself together after the last close call involving the deranged person coming around the sharp S-curve doing 150. He had headed straight toward us, finally swerving at the last minute to avoid hitting us.

I had decided that this whole driving thing was a game with the Italians. For me, it was looking more like a lose-lose situation. I was beginning to wonder how Angelo – or anyone for that matter – ever reached the age of 45 if he drove a car.

I was still trying to swallow my heart as we approached the upcoming rest stop, which looked to have only a few amenities.

"Well, I guess there's a bathroom. You can use it first," I remarked. "I'll stay in the car so that we don't have to lock it and roll up the windows. It's already hot in here."

"Okay, thanks," she agreed, finally loosening her grasp on the handle and throwing the door open, relieved to exit the death trap to which we had been assigned.

Ungluing my hands from the steering wheel, I got out

of the car. I was thrilled to plant my feet on firm ground and breathe fresh air rather than exhaust fumes from passing Italian cars.

I walked to the edge of the mountain and sat on a bench. They actually had put up a guardrail here. Why here and not on the cow path on which I had just driven? Slowly, I focused on the beautiful Italian village far below. Houses crept up the mountainside as the town overflowed its boundaries. A small, clear lake sat off to the edge of the village, throwing sparkles of light into my eyes. I wondered what people did for a living in the middle of nowhere. No grape vineyards in sight, no sheep or cattle, no farmland. I sat for perhaps ten minutes, my taut muscles starting to relax a bit when my thoughts were interrupted by Dee's return.

"What took you so long?" I inquired. I hoped that while she was gone, she had found not only a bathroom but also something for us to drink.

"I had to take off my shoes, socks, and jeans," she answered, trying to suppress a smile.

"What in the heck are you talking about, Dee?" I asked, confused but nonetheless curious.

"Well, there's just a hole in the ground, and I didn't want to get anything wet," she answered, her smug smile turning into a burst of laughter.

"You're kidding," I said in astonishment.

"No, I'm serious. That was it – a hole in the ground. Cross my heart." She *was* serious. I'm sure my face showed the horror I was feeling.

We had seen a million different kinds of toilets with hundreds of way to flush them, but never just a hole.

"Well, I'm not going in there," I remarked quickly. "I'll wait."

"It could be a long time before we find another bathroom," she commented. "Are you sure?"

"Yeah, Dee. *I'll wait.*"

We still had another hour of driving before we were out of the mountains. The scenery was fantastic – at least that's what Dee said. Her description of the valleys below sounded incredible, but my eyes were glued to the Boy Scout path that the Italians called a road. Clouds were rolling in, and I feared I'd have to compete with not only the road and crazy drivers, but also a storm and blinding rain. Images of disaster filled my mind.

Dee and I chatted about the villages in which her grandparents had lived. "I'm so anxious to see them," Dee confided. "You know that my grandmother told us stories when we were little of going to the creek and washing out their clothes. Her mother had ten children and all of the older girls had to help do the housework. When she met Grandpa, and their parents agreed to the marriage, she was thrilled to be out of the house with so many duties." Dee laughed. "And then she had twelve children of her own and had even more responsibilities."

"Were all their children born in Italy?" I questioned.

"No, the first two were, and then they got onto a freighter bound for America while Grandma was pregnant with the third. That was my Uncle Marco. My dad was born in the States. My mother's parents moved to America before any of the children were born so all of my mom's siblings were born in America."

I could feel the excitement in Dee's voice as we got closer and closer to our destination. Being from a close, extended Italian family, this trip meant a great deal to her, and I was so glad that we had taken the opportunity to drive to the villages, even though I questioned from time to time as to why I had gotten behind the wheel in this country that seemingly had no driving rules.

I could feel that we were slowly descending as my ears started to pop, and the incline became more and more slanted. Suddenly, out of nowhere, a small Italian village sprang up in a mountain clearing. It was comprised of perhaps forty old but well-kempt stucco houses with balconies, a hotel, café, general store, and gas station.

"Thank goodness. We've reached civilization, and there are a café and gas station," I said enthusiastically. My first thought was finding a bathroom – and fast. I prayed it wouldn't be a hole in the ground, and it wasn't.

Sitting in the shade at an outdoor wrought-iron table at the small cafe, we drank apricot juice and ate a cold pasta salad with crusty, Italian bread. Hungry and tired, I thought it was the best meal I had ever eaten. Robins and finches investigated the crumbs at our feet, and we threw them remnants of our meal. A young waitress understanding very little English poked her head outside occasionally, and we'd shake our heads "no" and smile. After sitting an hour, I still continued to savor my food as slowly as possible, dreading the thought of what was looming ahead of us on the roads to Todi.

It was then that I decided to spring a question on Dee. It was as good a time as ever while we were sitting in the safety of the café. No cars buzzing around us and no desperate three-mile drop-offs with no guardrails.

"Dee, we're on the back roads. There's not much traffic. There are more cows, sheep, and goats crossing the roads than there are cars driving. How about taking the wheel?" I pleaded. I knew it was a long shot to hope that she'd drive, but it was worth a try.

"The road is awfully narrow," she pointed out, as if I hadn't noticed.

"Oh, it's not bad at all," I lied. "Want to try?"

"Well, I don't know. Do you think that you can handle the navigation?"

I threw her a glance. She's serious, I thought.

"Well, I'll give it my *best* attempt, Dee. You may have to help me, though," I answered, covering the sarcasm.

"Well, okay. Let's buy gas, and then I'll take over."

We finished our second glass of juice and paid the bill.

I drove the car to the gas station next to the café. Approaching the pumps, we noticed there were different prices.

"Let's get the cheapest," I suggested.

"My thoughts exactly."

Even in the '70s, it was self-service everywhere in Europe. Of course, neither of us had ever pumped gas in those days, and, in addition, we couldn't read the Italian directions on the pumps. However, our main problem was that we couldn't insert the nozzle from the gas line into our gas tank. It was too large. We watched everyone else inserting the nozzle with no trouble. I held it in my hand, turning it over to examine it on all sides. It was just too big. I surveyed the opening to the gas tank on our Opal – it had a small opening and there was no way an over-sized nozzle was going to fit.

"So what's the trick to this? I don't get it." I remarked more to myself than to Dee. She had decided to be the spectator again and watch me make a fool of myself.

It seemed impossible to me that the Italians could be idiots on the highway and still know the trick of getting gas.

After five minutes of unsuccessful attempts of inserting the nozzle into our gas tank – I must have thought it would finally shrink and suddenly pop into the tank's opening – a kind-looking Italian gentleman approached us. "Are you having trouble?"

"Yes. Why won't this fit?" I asked, pointing to the nozzle and hoping that I didn't sound too stupid.

"You have a rental car, yes?"

"Yeah, we do," Dee interjected. "Is that a problem?"

"The rental cars take the gas at the other pump. It's more expensive, but the – how do you call that?" he asked, pointing to the object in my hand.

"Nozzle," I replied.

"Yes, the nozzle will fit," he smiled to us, pointing to a pump that was void of all Italian cars – no wonder, I thought, as I looked at the price listed above the pump.

"Oh, thank you, sir," I returned his smile.

"That's a crock," I whispered to Dee. "We have to buy the expensive gas. Look at the price." She nodded, returning to the map to take a final look.

I pulled the car to the other pump and filled the tank. The price was twice the cost of the gas at the first pump, but apparently we had no choice. Dee rounded the car, cleaning the windshield, plastered with bugs and mud.

As the gas pump shut off, I looked at the price. "The cost is 35,000 lira which is nearly thirty dollars to fill up. Thank goodness it's a small car, and we can go a long way on one tank of gas."

"Wow, I didn't know it'd be that expensive. I can fill up for five dollars back home," Dee added.

I walked inside the station with a credit card and returned to the car, ready to be a "passenger." Dee got behind the wheel, making her first attempt at European driving. With few cars on the road and the countryside flat, Dee decided that driving wasn't bad at all.

"It's certainly easier than navigating," she commented. "Being the navigator was really getting on my nerves. Glad that you decided to give it a try."

I resolved that the best thing to do was to keep my mouth shut.

For the first time, I realized how hot it was in the car. I started to scrutinize the dashboard.

"What are you doing?" Dee asked.

"Well, I know there's no air-conditioning in the car, but maybe there's a vent to blow air in. Or maybe a fan. It's really hot, don't you think?"

"Yeah and the sun is shining on your side of the car, which makes it..."

Dee never finished the sentence because suddenly a light began to flash on the dashboard.

"What's that?" Dee asked, as if I had a clue.

"Don't know."

My first thoughts were that we were overheated and the radiator needed water. Maybe the engine was on fire! I didn't know, but I realized that our luck wasn't usually good. My stomach was already tightening as I searched for an explanation for the flashing light.

"Pull over when you can, Dee." I tried to sound calm. I definitely didn't want the driver to panic.

Within the next few minutes, we saw a sign for a rest area, and Dee pulled off. By then, I had gotten the manual out of the glove compartment, but, of course, it was all in Italian.

A young couple with their three children were having a picnic at the roadside table, and as Dee continued to survey the dashboard, I bolted over to the couple, hoping for help. I remember wondering how to pantomime a "flashing light," but from the look on my face, the man must have known we were in trouble.

Following me to the car, he looked in. He, too, seemed confused. Suddenly, a light went on in my head. In searching for a button for a fan, I had pushed the red triangle, located in the middle of the dashboard. In *all* cars, the red triangle is for the emergency flashers! How could I have been so stupid, I thought.

Now, trying to act casual, I reached over and pushed the red triangle again, and the flashing light went off. Sheepishly, I smiled to the man and murmured "grazie."

"Gosh, I can't believe I turned on the flashers myself," I said when the man was out of earshot. "Well, one more crazy thing to add to my list," I grinned.

Dee giggled as she resumed her place behind the wheel. "Well, we both have a long list of nutty things we've done. They're all part of our European adventure, J.J."

During the next hour on the way to Todi, I had the first real opportunity to view the breathtaking scenery. Green hills dotted the landscape, and the hills in the distance were all topped with castles or ruins. Monasteries and nunneries also sat high on hills, with their church steeples reaching skyward and their bell towers sounding out the hour.

As we traveled through the vast countryside, lavish villas sprang up from time to time in the velvety green valleys. Brick walls surrounding them kept unwanted eyes from seeing, and we could only view small portions of the villa as we drove over slightly elevated regions of the land. We'd crane our necks to see the gorgeous flower gardens, immaculate and picture-perfect in blooms of red, purple, blue, orange and yellow. The vast layout of the buildings – usually white stucco – gave opportunity for dozens of wrought-iron balconies. Chimneys topped every room, and pools and fountains adorn the perfectly manicured landscape. We wondered if they housed extended families or maybe they were private resorts.

In addition to the villas, we also came across many quaint villages nestled in the plush valleys, surrounded by nearby mountains, snow-capped and awesome. The traditional stucco houses – painted various colors of yellow, orange, blue, and pink – all sported balconies and window boxes overflowing with flowers. Tiny, winding streets ran through the towns, always at an incline, and numerous small – possibly family-owned – stores seemed to inhabit each village. Certainly, these small towns as well as the castles, monasteries, and nunneries threw us directly back into medieval days.

It was late afternoon when we finally arrived in Todi and were proud that we had successfully survived our first day on the highways of Italy. Todi was one of the most picturesque Italian towns we had visited, nestled on a high hill overlooking the Tiber Valley. Arcades and pale yellow houses with stone-shingled roofs framed a perfect town square. Wrought-iron balconies – each containing flower boxes full of red, blooming geraniums – decorated each of the fourteenth-century homes. Two bronze equestrian statues towered over a lavish Baroque fountain in the middle of the square. The town immediately won our hearts with its ancient, uncorrupted medieval air.

We located a hotel on a winding road leading out of town. It was a village inn – small, homey, and comfortable. The bedroom was painted and decorated primarily in white with shear curtains at the windows. A small balcony with wicker chairs was an added attraction as we opened the French doors to let the afternoon breeze fill the room.

Even though we were exhausted from the trials and tribulations of a day on the roads of Italy, our thoughts were on our mission. We unpacked and quickly exited our room in search of answers to the Delmastro family history and their life in Todi.

Chapter 21

Christina Maria

We went first in search of old cemeteries, locating one on the outskirts of town with gravestones in all sizes – six foot tall to tiny headstones constructed especially for babies.

One of the most beautiful tombstones we saw had pink and yellow roses intricately carved beside inlaid oval pictures of two little girls. Mosaics of pink marble adorned the sides of the white tombstone with carved green ivy trailing down the edges. Two vases full of sprays of yellow, red, and blue blossoms stood at the foot of the grave. I felt tears swell in my eyes as I realized that these tiny girls died together one year earlier – perhaps in a car accident or fire.

Many of the gravesites were hundreds of years old and so corroded that the inscriptions were illegible. Despite the age of the cemetery, it was well kept. The Italians' love of flowers was seen at nearly every grave. Potted plants and fresh-cut flowers blossomed throughout the cemetery.

We located several Delmastro gravesites that were intact and legible – Regina and Mario, Emelia and Alfredo, Paola and Antonio, and a single stone for little Albino. All had resting dates of a century earlier. Dee snapped pictures, hoping they were relatives that someone in her family might recognize.

Dee and I talked to a few people – shopkeepers mostly – who spoke English, searching for anyone who had known any Delmastros. Going into an antique shop in the middle of town, we searched through old sepia photographs. Many had no names or dates on the back, but two had Delmastro plainly printed, and we rejoiced that Dee had something tangible to take home.

Our last afternoon, we sat in a tiny outdoor café, a bit downhearted that we hadn't found more of Dee's heritage. The pretty young Italian waitress, dressed in her proper black dress and white lace apron, brought us each a slice of cake along with strong, dark expresso coffee.

Her English seemed decent, so I asked on a whim, "Miss, we are looking for clues to my friend's heritage. Her family was from Todi," I said pointing to Dee. "Do you know anyone by the name of Delmastro?"

"Delmastro?" she repeated in a soft, husky voice. "Is that your last name?" she asked, looking at Dee. She was petite with beautiful, strong facial features that all blended perfectly with the husky whisper.

"Yes. Do you know anyone by that name?"

The waitress thought for a second. "No, but my grandmother has lived in Todi for eighty years. She might. I get off work in half an hour. If you can wait, I'm taking food to her, and you can go along."

It was an offer we couldn't resist, and Dee's eyes lit up at the suggestion.

"That would be great. Thank you," Dee answered, excitedly.

Her name was Christina Maria. When she came back to our table half an hour later, she had changed from her work clothes into a soft, flowering dress. She was carrying a tray of food, and her shoulder-length black hair bounced with every step she made.

We walked with her through the village, towards her grandmother's house, passing dozens of shops, cafes, and office buildings until we came to the main square – *Piazza del Popolo*. The square looked like a postcard of uncorrupted medieval days with a thirteenth-century Roman temple at one end. We continued to a sleepy corner of Todi on the outskirts and took a small wooden bridge across a clear blue stream lined with huge old oak trees.

Christina Maria's grandmother had a room in a fourteenth-century building made into apartments. Climbing to the second floor, Grandmother Rosa was waiting at the door with a hug and kiss. A stout, white-haired lady with sparkling black eyes, she certainly didn't look her eighty years.

Christina explained in rapid Italian who we were, and Rosa extended kisses to us as well – one on each cheek, Italian style. Christina placed her grandmother's food on a plate, continuing her discussion in Italian. The conversation flowed easily from Italian to English as Christina relayed her grandmother's thoughts to us.

"She remembers Giovanni Delmastro," Christina finally said softly. "He owned a grocery store that my grandmother used to go to as a child."

"Oh, gosh, that would have been my grandfather," Dee replied, choking back tears of excitement.

"My grandmother says that he was a wonderful man. He had two children when he and his wife, Domenica, moved to America. Domenica was originally from up north somewhere, Grandmother thinks. It was an arranged marriage, and no one in Todi ever got to know Domenica well."

"Domenica. Yes...yes, that was my grandmother. I was named after her. Domenica Francesca." Dee was silent for a moment. "And those two children were my uncles." Tears were starting to roll down her cheeks. "The older child died on the boat to America, but the younger of the boys was Josef. He was and still is my favorite uncle."

Christina translated Dee's words into Italian, and her grandmother smiled broadly as she realized that she had known some of Dee's family.

Again, Christina Maria was listening to her grandmother's rapid Italian, smiling and nodding her head. "She says she used to play with Theresa Delmastro when she was about six or so. Theresa's family had moved here from Milano. They lived on the same street as my grandmother.

She thinks Theresa's father was a cousin to Giovanni."

"Really?" Dee said excitedly. "Does she still live around here?"

"No, they only stayed in Todi for two years or so and then moved south. My grandmother says she loved Theresa – such a frail little child with huge black eyes. They were together everyday for those two years. After she moved, my grandmother never heard from her again."

Christina Maria laughed as her grandmother rattled on. "Grandmother Rosa says that she and Theresa used to sneak into the wine vineyards on the hillsides and pick grapes to eat. One day they ate hundreds of red grapes. They were both sick that night, and it was months before my grandmother could stand to eat another red grape."

Grandmother Rosa's face beamed as she remembered the days of her childhood, her eyes sparkling as she exhaled her hearty laugh. We sat for an hour exchanging information with her – Dee told Rosa about her uncles, aunts and father and then jotted down information to take home to her parents. It was a fantastic experience for Dee.

Rosa seemed to enjoy reminiscing, continuing to spew forth recollections long tucked away in her memory. Rosa told what it was like growing up in a poor village that had little to offer to its residents. People struggled to find work and feed large families. Children went to grammar school if parents could afford it, but many started work in the vineyards at age ten or twelve. Amazingly, though, many of those children stayed after they were grown and married to raise their own families in the same surroundings. The love of their country and devotion to their roots kept them in Todi.

As it neared 10 p.m., we graciously thanked Rosa for sharing her evening with us. Remarkably, she returned the thanks to us for spending time with her, reminiscing about old times.

Christina Maria walked us back through town, pointing

242

out several places of which her grandmother had spoken. The building – which had been Dee's grandfather's grocery store with living quarters above it – now contained various government offices. She showed us the tiny church where the family had worshipped and the building, which formerly acted as a grammar school for all children in Todi. Dee's grandparents undoubtedly had spent some of their early days there.

A notebook full of facts and a roll of film later, our evening with Christina Maria was concluded. She kissed both of us as she held our hands, thanking us for a wonderful evening. Looking at Dee's face, I knew it was a momentous event that she would never forget and one that we reminisced about for years to come – our night in Todi with Christina Maria and Grandmother Rosa.

Chapter 22

Arrivederci, Europa

We left for Assisi the next morning with high hopes of finding similar information about the Simoncini family – her mother's ancestors. However, we found no "Christina Maria" to help us. Searching St. Maria's Cemetery in Assisi, we found Simoncini graves, snapping pictures of all of them in hopes that Dee's mother would recognize some of the names.

We continued to talk to people we met, hoping that someone would remember the Simoncinis, but Dee's mother's family had left Italy a generation before the Delmastros, and we continually were met with no success.

We finally decided just to enjoy the beautiful sights of the medieval town with its geranium-hung main street, the fountain-splashed piazzas, and its breathtaking view of green hillsides and pure blue skies.

We had strolled through the winding stone streets, focusing on the many ancient but beautiful houses. Some were two-story with several upper-level balconies, opening into airy bedrooms. Mostly constructed from the yellow clay of the region, some retained their original color while others were painted a brilliant white or a pale pink.

We visited the magnificent historic *Basilica di San Francesco,* built for St. Francis of Assisi in 1228, two years after his death. Over the next century, some of Italy's foremost artists – Cimabue, Simone Martini, Pietro Lorenzetti, and Giotto – decorated both the Upper and Lower Church. Being one of the Christian world's greatest shrines, many of the frescoes depicted the life of St. Francis. Cimabue painted many simple paintings, capturing the humility of the revered saint who represented poverty, chastity, and obedience while Lorenzettti created a bold fresco based on the twisted figure of Christ on the cross.

Hundreds of white stone steps led to the Upper Church, which housed a glorious sanctuary. The gorgeous soaring arches in the sanctuary were built to symbolize the heavenly glory depicted by St. Francis' life. These extraordinarily high arches later influenced all Franciscan churches.

Totally elated by the cathedral, Dee and I left the Basilica, knowing that many of her ancestors must have visited that church regularly as had thousands of pilgrims. Even though we were unable to find any significant information about her mom's family, Dee didn't feel dejected. She had succeeded beyond a doubt in Todi, which was enough to make our trip to the Umbria region successful. Regrettably, we left that spectacular, peaceful area of Italy and regained access onto the highway – still full of maniacs – all leading toward Rome. I decided to take the main road rather than chance getting lost on the mountain trails. We had three days before we needed to be in Rome.

Within the next three days, we received a parking ticket in a village while eating lunch, ended up in a soccer field while trying to find a city center, and needed the local police to direct us to the main highway when we were lost. In a hotel, Dee somehow got locked in a bathroom – which was shared by the entire floor – for an hour during the middle of the night; while *I* slept in bed, *she* slept on the bathroom floor. On the last day, I dropped my bottle of precious Paris perfume in the hallway while showing it to a fellow traveler, and the entire floor smelled of "La Joie Parfum" the several days. "I didn't have room for it in my luggage anyway" was my way of laughing instead of crying.

The last day on the road, a battle with a giant bumblebee ensued when it decided to share our car. In the middle of a high bridge, which closed the gap of an immense gorge, the bee decided to join us. Not liking heights or bees, it was a challenge to maintain my sanity and drive to safety. Of course, it was only one of many frantic moments since I had gotten behind the wheel of the little red Opal. Buzzing around the car, the bee finally found its way out an open window as Dee swung her jacket about the car to direct it in the right direction.

Nearing Rome, Dee and I started reminiscing about the crazy experiences we had encountered on our European vacation of '72.

"Dee, just think of all of the adventures we've had on this trip – getting stuck at the top of the Eiffel Tower, sleeping on the floor of a night train to Spain, and nearly getting a free shower in the porta-potty in Paris." I could almost hear Dee's giggles over the roar of the black Fiat that was passing me at a record-breaking speed. I was used to the craziness now and just continued my spiel.

"And how about nearly getting picked up by the Italian police or climbing the staircase-to-hell in Amsterdam?" I asked.

Dee was cackling. "You know, J.J., the funniest thing – *now*, but not then – was getting left behind in the train station in Madrid." Dee paused a second and changed her mind. "But it was also pretty funny seeing your face when you got the raw egg in your soup."

"Well, Dee, speaking of eggs, how about the picture of the wild animal I saw when I asked for eggs in France."

By now, Dee was wiping the tears from her eyes as she squealed with laughter about our escapades.

We chuckled all the way into Rome as we remembered the close calls and unforgettable memories we had had. Before returning our rental car, we found a hotel on the outskirts of town. We had decided not to return to "Angelo" because it was difficult enough to leave him the first time. Without seeing him, it would be easier to enjoy our last day in Rome.

We sloughed my brown and chartreuse bags and Dee's two black ones from the car into the hotel lobby. Dee had finished her souvenir shopping, buying Italian glass beaded bracelets for the remainder of her sisters. She wrapped them carefully and plunged them into her carry-on, which now had three "Italia" stickers plastered on its side. Everyone eyeing her bag knew that she loved Italy.

Many of my stickers had traveled the entire gamut of Europe and were looking rather war-torn. Taped and glued, they clung to my two bags in an attempt to get back to Illinois.

Our backseat had become a catchall as we purchased souvenirs, food, drinks, and candy. Everything – wrappers, empty juice cartons, banana peels, apple cores, and empty bags – were tossed into the back until it looked like a heap of garbage under, around, and covering our travel-stickered bags. Before finding a hotel, we located a dumpster and cleaned out the trash-filled rear seat and trunk.

Quickly registering at the hotel in Rome, we left our luggage in a storage room on the main floor, found directions to the car rental office, and got into our little red Opal that had come through 800 kilometers of the Indy 500 without a scratch.

Going into Rome seemed much easier than getting out because suddenly all of the one-way streets seemed to surprisingly lead toward the center. With only one wrong turn, we found our car rental office. Because we had spent our last four unnerving days in our red Opal, we felt a special attachment to her. She was dirty now after days on the back roads, but I snapped a picture of our trusty vehicle to which we had entrusted our lives on the highways of Italy. I knew I'd find a place of distinction in my photo album for the red Opal that had contributed to so many apprehensive as well as momentous highway episodes.

Walking the ten blocks to the hotel after returning our vehicle, I commented, "Dee, this has been a fantastic vacation. I hate to return to reality because..."

I didn't get to finish my thought because Dee interrupted me. "J.J., watch out! You're going to step in..."

Well, it was too late. My foot slipped into the unmentionable dog mess on the sidewalk. Dee was already chuckling as I stood plastered to the spot, trying to decide exactly what to do next. I had to smile as I looked at Dee, who seemed to be particularly enjoying the situation.

I searched my purse for Kleenex, knowing that even if I had a packet of tissues, there wouldn't be enough to tackle the job. The shoes were going to be left behind the next day anyway. Spying a garbage can, I fumbled with the laces, the only clean parts of the sneakers, and the shoes bit the dust with a loud thud.

* * * * * * * * *

Packing and repacking, discarding old clothes, and repacking again, we tried to find room for our latest souvenirs. Unsuccessful in closing our already fat, bulging, overweight luggage, we looked for more old clothes to throw away and attempted to re-pack again. When my neon carry-on refused to zipper shut, I pulled out the blue and yellow striped luggage strap to hold it closed.

"I loved having the car because we didn't have to pack everything into our luggage each night – we could just toss everything into the trunk or backseat. But it's a real problem now," Dee said, stuffing the last of her purchases into her carry-on. Hearing a final click, I knew she had succeeded in closing it.

We decided to go to the hotel lobby that night for a glass of wine to celebrate the end of our European adventure. We sat next to a young couple speaking Italian, but the gentleman continually glanced our way with a smile. He had fair complexion with blonde hair so he seemed out of place in a country of olive-skinned, dark-haired people. Struggling to interpret the Italian menu so that we could order a snack, he leaned his head over and whispered, "I'm an American. Maybe I can help you."

His name was John Vogelsang and his beautiful Italian wife was Clarissa. John had met her in Italy while on a business trip. They fell in love, got married, and John moved to Rome where the company for which he worked had a corporate office. He adored Italy, fitting into the culture and speaking the language as if he were a native. Clarissa spoke English well, too, so Dee and I enjoyed hearing of life in Italy from a young couple's perspective.

John and Clarissa had purchased an old, rundown farmhouse when they were married three years earlier. It was in the hills outside of Rome, and they had worked on restoring it, putting in electricity, tearing down walls and rebuilding them, replacing windows, piping running water, tiling the roof, and all the other necessities that go with modern living. They were nearly done now and had moved in six months earlier – all in due time as Clarissa was now two months pregnant.

As fate would have it, we were leaving the next day with no opportunity to see the restored farmhouse except visual images we had from their descriptions. In the weeks to come, we received photographs of "before and after," and when little Renaldo was born, we sent presents from the States to adorn the beautiful black-haired little prince. He had all of Clarissa dark features but had John's blue eyes and adoring smile. What a combination!

Again, as we departed that evening, we felt as if we had met friends that would have been lifelong had we lived in the same community, and regrettably we could only exchange addresses in hopes of meeting again someday.

Years later on a brief stay in Rome, I called the Vogelsangs and had the opportunity to see their gorgeous farmhouse that was fully restored by then with skylights, wooden ceiling beams, and a fantastic second-floor balcony, looking out onto the lush, green hillsides outside of Rome.

Best of all, I had the privilege of meeting Renaldo who was ten by then. What a handsome Italian-American he was! His Italian as well as his English was perfect, and he still possessed the dark hair and olive complexion of his mother and the blue eyes and endearing smile of his father. Without question he was a special young man and would steal the hearts of many girls in years to come.

* * * * * * * * * *

The next morning, we threw away the last of our shampoo, toothpaste, deodorant, and anything else that wouldn't fit into our purses – suitcases were permanently closed the night before, and no effort on earth could squeeze one more item into them. Our pajamas were left on the bed, and we pooled our Italian money, hoping to have enough to pay for a taxi to the airport.

While sitting on our room balcony and eating our last European breakfast of rolls, juice, and expresso coffee, Dee asked, "Do you think anyone will ever believe us when we tell them of our adventures? We had some incredible things happen to us, you know."

"Never! We had more remarkable experiences in Europe this one summer than most people have in a lifetime," I replied. "I'm so glad that I kept a detailed diary so I won't forget anything."

As the years passed, Dee and I reflected many times on the nine-week trip abroad, and slowly we began to realize the many things that we had gained from our adventures. It was not only a trip through Europe, but also a journey towards maturity and the initial stages to finding ourselves.

For me, it fueled my restless spirit so that I yearned to see more of the world, and through future travel, I was finally able to answer "Who am I?" More than just seeing the spectacular sights of the old world and surviving the incredible exploits that were thrown our way, we met so many intriguing people that taught us about life and ultimately about ourselves.

Lilly instilled in us the thought to smile through all circumstances and live life to the fullest while Hans showed us that you could travel the world, but you must go where your heart is in order to be happy. Then there was Tim, who helped us understand the feelings of Europeans who had suffered through the WWII and who now looked at Americans in a way that I hadn't conceived. We often talked of Sarah and her single-minded goal and task in life to be a Mormon and preach the Word of God. And, of course, our experience with Miep always reminded us of being humble, as she claimed that she hadn't done anything special in helping the Jews. Most importantly, we remembered Jean-Paul and Angelo, who unknowingly illustrated in their own way just how gorgeous Europeans truly are.

All in all, I believe, that both Dee and I would say that the one thing we learned from the European culture that remained with us for a long time was to be patient – we learned this, of course, during our mealtimes as we were eventually able to go with the flow of the old-world customs and enjoy people-watching as we waited for our food.

"J.J., I've been thinking," Dee remarked as we sat on the balcony. As much as you love to write, you should compile all of our escapades into a book. We've experienced some real adventures, but we've also learned some valuable lessons. I don't think that either of us is returning home the same person who left nine weeks ago."

Dee's idea raised my eyebrows. Without hesitation, I replied, "You know, Dee, that's a fantastic idea."

The seed was planted. "That's what I'll do someday, Dee. I'll write a book!" Dee smiled, taking a final sip of expresso coffee and picking up the phone to ask the hotel clerk to call a taxi.

"Right now, though, we need to get home. Within the next few weeks, we both will have a classroom full of kids waiting to learn – and many will be anxious to hear of our European adventures. They'll never believe the incredible experiences we had, and despite all, we visited Europe and survived!"

We both laughed as we tugged, dragged, and pushed our souvenir-filled suitcases into the hallway, taking one last glance at our final European hotel before closing the door.

"*Arrivederci, Roma*," Dee whispered. Glancing out of the corner of my eye, I noticed a tiny tear trickled down her cheek as she closed the door.

"It has been one heck of a vacation, J.J. One we'll *never* forget."

"You're right, Dee. *Arrivederci, Europa*," I added. "We'll be back someday. I promise."

Author's Biography

Jan Frazier

A former secondary English teacher, for many years Frazier took students abroad during the summers so that they could experience first-hand what Frazier had learned to love in 1972 – the amazing countries of old-world Europe. She acknowledges her love of travel in this novel, which is based on true-life experiences from her many exciting years of exploring Europe. Still traveling abroad, Frazier takes adults and college students during the summer months. She now teaches English and speech at Bradley University, Peoria, Illinois. Frazier has been honored for five consecutive years in *Who's Who Among American Teachers*.

CPSIA information can be obtained at www.ICGtesting.com
Printed in the USA
LVOW12s1336110914

403615LV00001B/24/P